ESSENCE OF REFLECTION

Essence of Reflection
Martial Arts and Life

Dan Popp

kamel press

Harrisburg, Pennsylvania
www.oikarate.org

Library of Congress Control Number: 2021951498

ISBN-13:
>   978-1-62487-073-6 – paperback
>   978-1-62487-074-3 – ebook

Published in the USA.

There is only one way to avoid criticism:
do nothing, say nothing and be nothing.

Aristotle

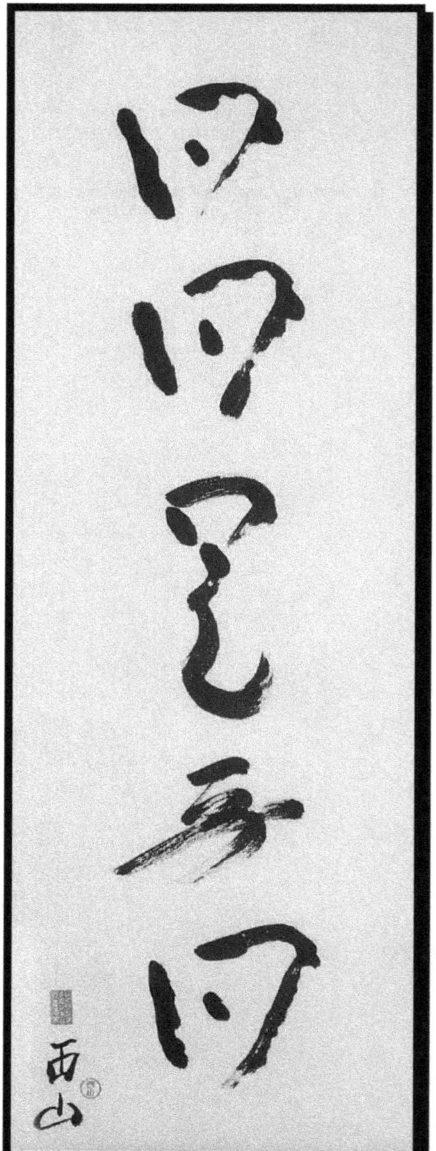
西山

Nichi Nichi Kore Konichi

Every Day is a Good Day

(calligraphy by the author)

"Many are deceived by 'good' and think that is the opposite of bad. Thus, many think that 'good day' means happy, beautiful day. Unmon (Zen master), however, did not mean it that way. Unmon's 'good day' is far more profound. He was pointing to right here, right now, unprecedented, unrepeatable, absolute day."

Eido Tai Shimano

Zen Word, Zen Calligraphy

DEDICATION

To my daughters, my martial arts students, and to all with an interest to improve themselves. May these topics and reflections serve as reminders that you are capable of more than you realize. Keep setting goals and keep working relentlessly until you reach them.

As always, to my martial arts instructors:

Toby Cooling – Order of Isshin-Ryu Karate
Rick Manglinong – SMP Arnis
Isham Latimer – Chi-Ryu Jiujitsu
Dave Joyner – Kendo

ACKNOWLEDGMENTS

My first thank you, for everything I have and anything I ever will achieve, is for my savior, Jesus Christ. Without Him, nothing is possible.

To my family for their continuous support and encouragement. My daughters, Britteni and Kayla, you both are growing to be strong, independent women for whom I am so very proud. Always set goals and pursue them relentlessly. Those efforts will lead you toward your dreams.

To the Order of Isshin-Ryu and Sining Marsiyal ng Pilipinas (SMP) Arnis families. It is an honor and privilege to train and grow alongside all of you. My wish is that we travel along the same path together for many years to come.

As always, I must recognize and pay respect to each of my martial arts instructors: Toby Cooling (Order of Isshin-Ryu), Rick Manglinong (Kombatan, Modern Arnis), Isham Latimer (Chi-Ryu Jiujitsu), and Dave Joyner (Kendo).

A special thank you to Grand Master Toby Cooling, founder of the Order of Isshin-Ryu in 1971, for providing the Foreword to this publication.

A nod also to Master Diane Ortenzio-Cooling. A highly accomplished martial artist and competitor, you provided the inspiration for the chapter titled Competition after your recent seminar on kata competition insights for the Order of Isshin-Ryu.

Thank you to Master John Costanzo for the design and graphics work on the front and back cover of this book.

Thank you to Sheryl Z Photography for your amazing talent and generous usage of your photo of Kayla (see chapter titled Observation). See Sheryl's website: https://www.sherylzphotography.com/

Thanks again to the Kamel Press team. Working with you always makes the writing process run smoothly and efficiently and your results always exceed my expectations.

TABLE of CONTENTS

FOREWORD

Very seldom does one come upon a work with the depth that Dan Popp has included in this book. Dan has assembled a fantastic reference to a way of life that is the martial arts.

Martial arts are sometimes depicted as something one "does" for exercise, self-defense, or some other benefit. While those are definite bonuses in the training, there are those who follow the martial arts as a way of life that enables a transformation into a better version of themselves.

While I have been Dan's main instructor for over 25 years, he has studied with other instructors in several disciplines. He is a keen observer and delves deeply into whatever he has been shown in order to understand it fully and from different perspectives. This book is the culmination of that deep perspective, and he shares that work with us now to benefit others who also walk the path of martial arts.

It is with great pleasure and pride that I recommend this work.

Toby Cooling
Founder, Order of Isshin-Ryu
November 2, 2021

INTRODUCTION

There is a book that is most likely a part of every serious martial artist's personal library: *Zen in the Martial Arts*, by Joe Hyams. This book was published in 1979 by Tarcher and subsequently in 1982 by Bantam, which is the version in my library. I started my martial arts journey in 1982; therefore, this book was fresh off the presses when I started my own library of books covering many topics on the arts. *Zen in the Martial Arts* provides a variety of short stories by the author, covering his experiences in learning several martial arts from famous practitioners such as Bruce Lee, Larry Tatum, Ed Parker, and Bong Soo Han. These stories of Hyams' experiences provide a glimpse into the mindset of these genuine martial artists and others, along with anecdotes on Zen-like approaches to life. Being 15 years old at the time of reading this book, it strongly impacted my approach to training and provided a valuable resource for me.

Fast forward to now, and I recall recommending this book to many of my students over the years. Each one fully absorbed the content of that publication and were appreciative of the recommendation as they expressed how much they enjoyed reading it, over and over. To my knowledge, in the four decades since, no one has published another book similar in style to *Zen in the Martial Arts*. A book of various topics relating to martial arts training as well as general self-improvement areas in a format that the reader can go back and refer to over and over again. This inspired me to move forward with this project. These are topics I've been jotting down for the past 15 years or so. These are meant to serve as my experiences and reflections for others to consider in their training.

My wish is to be a small part of the advancement of the arts, a piece of the ongoing puzzle to further improve the mind and the thought processes in your martial arts training. The golfer Ben Hogan expressed in his book *The Modern Fundamentals of Golf,* "I hope that these lessons will serve as a body of knowledge that will lead to further advances in our understanding of the golf swing. Every year we learn a little more about golf. Each new chunk of valid knowledge paves the way to greater knowledge." This summarizes the idea behind this publication. To assist you in your pursuit of more knowledge and under-standing. As always, I encourage my fellow martial artists to consider doing the same. There is a wealth of knowledge and experience out there that could benefit future generations of martial artists immensely. I look forward to your efforts and adding your title to my personal library to help me become a better martial artist. I hope you enjoy these reflections. God bless.

Dan Popp
Harrisburg, Pennsylvania
October 15, 2021

SPACE: THE STARING POINT

Beginning students of martial arts, regardless of style, start out their journey with instructions on proper stances and postures, how to deliver the various strikes and blocks of their respective style, and general rules of the dojo or training hall. These are all needed to progress and develop as a practitioner of the martial arts and to move on to more advanced concepts and training drills. Once these skills are developed to a point of confidence, students then begin to explore more subtle concepts of the arts. One of the first and most important being that of understanding and commanding space.

Space, for many, is the true starting point of training or the focus of the one thing to work on and improve. You must know your spacing. Improve your understanding and control of space, and you will be well on your way to improvement in martial arts.

A question for you to consider and reflect is the following: Have some modern styles of martial arts moved away from teaching close range techniques? For a minute imagine a student, or even an advanced black belt, who trains in the same system without ever exploring another art. In theory, you are exposed only to the techniques of that system and the interpretations and boundaries of those same techniques. If we look at the punching and kicking of many modern systems of martial arts, the techniques are all delivered at full length or range of motion. For example, a kick delivered within the kata, or fighting form, is performed with a full extension of the foot to a target that is envisioned at the point where the leg is at full extension. This is practiced over and over, yet we realize the odds of a kick delivered in this fashion in a true fighting situation may be quite low. Why do modern systems emphasize strikes at full-length of delivery?

Exposure to various styles of martial arts provides a great way to develop a solid understanding of space and how space affects the delivery of offensive or defensive techniques. The arts from the Philippines deploy a variety of stick and blade techniques, and all of them contain techniques from the three general ranges of fighting: close, medium, and long. Another consideration for exposure to different ranges of fighting are the Chinese systems such as Wing Chun. My exposure includes the art of Liuhebafa as included within a modern system of jiujitsu called Chi-Ryu Jiujitsu. This system incorporates self-defense training drills comprised of a few techniques, called movements, whereby your techniques are delivered at very close range to your opponent. Liuhebafa is a very old Chinese system of martial arts. The techniques are very close range and are extremely effective. So, I wonder, why are many systems emphasizing strikes at longer ranges?

We know from history and various sources that at a certain point in time, the idea was to get martial arts into a more mainstream position in society due to the benefits of training such as mental focus, spiritual development, and physical improvement. The founder of Judo, Jigoro Kano, and modern karate, Gichin Funakoshi, both systematized the techniques and requirements for rank to make these arts more accessible to all people. The movements were modified from a *jitsu* (application) to a *do* (way or path) to make training safer for everyone. Arguably, the application's effectiveness was modified as well as space, an integral part of an application's success, was somewhat removed from the instruction.

The student of martial arts needs to be aware of these historical changes. You need to research, explore, and, if available, study other styles and systems for a more complete assessment of how space is utilized in your development as a martial artist. The famous Japanese swordsman Miyamoto Musashi writes in *The Book of Five Rings*, his treatise of martial arts, the following regarding space and reversal, "The way to win in a battle according to military science is to know the rhythms of the specific opponents, and use rhythms that your opponents do not expect..." With his sword, Musashi eventually realized from studying space closely that his techniques lacked effectiveness at close range more than they did at 'normal' or longer ranges. He adapted and developed a system whereby his short sword was deployed at close ranges, when needed. He then had techniques available from long range all the way to very close range since he had a strong command of his space.

Obviously, your understanding and control of space will develop over many years of training. Everyone starts from somewhere. I had a beginning Kendo student who competed in a tachi-ai, or competition. He had only been training for about a year at this time. Before his first match, I pulled him aside and informed him his opponent was more advanced. My advice was to make sure he kept a good bit of space between himself and his opponent. This way, he would force his opponent to make the effort to try to score. Considering the extra space maintained, my student would have an extra split second to block and attempt a counterattack. I told him this strategy would keep him in the match much longer than if he stayed at a distance that his opponent was hoping for – which is where the shinai, or bamboo swords, cross near the end.

During the course of the match, there was quite a few attempts by the opponent to score but to no avail as my student was able to block and the opponent could not execute a clean striking technique. After each attempt, my student quickly separated and created the extended spacing. At one point, my student was able to score a point to his opponent's *kote*, or wrist area. My student ended up winning his first match 1-0. He was unable to fare as well for his second match but he walked away that day with a good perspective on how space can be utilized to neutralize a more skilled opponent.

The concept of understanding space applies to whatever sport or activity you are trying to win. Take wrestling as an example. Successful wrestlers not only know their skills thoroughly, but they also study their opponents. Often, you will notice the wrestlers tend to hold back and circle the opponent without committing to a specific offensive move. It is at these times the wrestler is being cautious and observant and simply picking up cues on space and how his opponent is using space – good or bad – to take advantage of his opponent at the right moment. Space is a huge component of a successful wrestler's toolbox. Although the space under consideration for them is much shorter than a Kendo match, the concepts remain the same.

Students of martial arts should be encouraged to study various arts to gain a more well-rounded experience, understanding, and respect for the concept of space. Get out of your comfort zone and experience how space is affected when applying techniques from different arts. Difficulty in execution of techniques from another system, or even failure of those techniques is not a bad thing. It means you are learning more and more about space. And that, in the end, will make you a better martial artist.

BALANCE. BREATH. VISION.

Three critical components of any martial art or approach to self-defense are balance, breath, and vision. The control of these facets of an engagement are relevant whether you are trying to manage them for yourself or trying to overtake them in your adversary.

My karate sensei, Grandmaster Toby Cooling of the Order of Isshin-Ryu, provided this lesson at my studio about 25 years ago. He was demonstrating a technique from a wrist grab with one of my students serving as his *uke*, or self-defense partner. Most often, techniques are performed to quickly strike and hopefully end the situation. As everyone anticipated, he immobilized my student's grab and executed and upper cut style strike to the ribs.

My sensei asked everyone, "Is the fight over?" We all sort of nodded and responded that it appeared that way, yes. Grandmaster Cooling then informed us, "Well, maybe. What if this guy was twice this size and was a seasoned fighter, and could take a good punch?"

He then repeated the technique but this time he added a front leg sweep which unbalanced my student quite a bit. He then explained to all of us, "I obviously increased the effectiveness of my defensive technique there, but there's another piece to this puzzle which will all but guarantee I dominate my opponent." Sensei continued, "What if I can also take away his vision in the process of my movements?"

With my student's balance being affected after being struck to the ribs, Grandmaster Cooling performed a *shuto*, or open hand strike, to the partner's face and held it there. This strike caused his head to turn away from the action. He then said to the student, "Go ahead and fight back." There was nothing my student could do at that point. He was completely unable to retaliate in any way.

The demonstration shows that to attain victory, you must control or dominate all three of these attributes in your opponent. Controlling or gaining the upper hand in one or two of them and you have a good chance; however, a seasoned fighter has ability and chance to readjust. Take control of all three and you are clearly in control. Think of each one as having one-third importance in the overall equation. Win two out of three and your chances are good, but it's still only 66 percent.

Have you noticed that police officers always apply handcuffs from behind the person? They want to be in a position where the person cannot see them; therefore, they have greatly reduced strength. Think of military strategy where an attack occurs from the flank. It is difficult to defend against as you cannot see the other side directly.

In terms of the samurai, Musashi always wanted the sunlight to his back. He wanted his adversary looking directly into the sun so that it was difficult to see Musashi clearly.

11

Boxers train relentlessly to control the breathing aspect of their craft. They put in long hours with bag work and running to bring their cardio up to high tolerance levels. They know that having any chance to last during a 12-round fight will take a lot of cardiovascular development, so they train this aspect very hard.

They also train on the ability to take punches to the midsection. They know that if they don't develop their core section and learn to expel their breath at just the right time when a punch is imminent, they will lose control over their breath and give the opponent the upper hand in the bout.

The art of Kendo also forces control over your breath; otherwise, improvement will come very slowly. Watch a Kendo match closely. Yes, there are flashes of strong techniques and striking to various parts of the armor worn by the participants. But at all other times you must be in control over your breathing. If not, you will tend to inhale and exhale strongly, which leads the tip of your shinai, or bamboo sword, to move up and down with your breathing. The experienced Kendo-ka will rapidly notice and take advantage by striking during the inhale or exhale when your mind is preoccupied with your heavy breathing, thus giving you no chance to react in time.

Balance is a requirement of any martial art or sport. The main objective for football players is to unbalance the opposing team. A defensive player who doesn't make a tackle was unable to unbalance the ball carrier. They are taught to wrap up the runner from the hips and down. Arm tackles are highly unsuccessful, and they do not create unbalance in the runner's effort.

In martial arts, the key is movement. As my sensei in Chi-Ryu Jiujitsu, master Isham Latimer, explains, "The genesis of any solid technique is movement." Only through moving do you have a chance to unbalance your opponent. If you remain locked in a particular stance while your opponent is moving, it becomes next to impossible to unbalance your opponent."

Think of all three concepts – balance, breath, vision – in your training. Consider them from not only your perspective to control them, but also from your adversary's perspective and how to take them away. This reflection and struggle apply in every aspect of your life: work, play, and hobbies. When I'm engaged in my painting, I need to have control over by balance, breath, and vision. If one of those aspects is not in line with the others, my progress with the piece I'm working on will suffer. I always need to be aware of them to produce something that meets my expectations.

OBSERVATION

Observation is one aspect of martial arts training that is often overlooked. Everything and potentially every situation is a learning opportunity if you observe closely. Professional athletes take the skill of observation well beyond the normal level. That's how, in large part, they were able to reach the professional level in the first place.

If you watch a major league baseball game, you'll see the players in the dugout watch the opposing pitcher very closely. They are looking for any clue or repeated motion that will indicate the pitch that is about to be thrown. That's part of their job. They need to find any hint of a tell-tale sign on what the pitcher may be throwing to give them an upper hand when they are at bat. This is no different than a professional poker player.

Whatever clue that can be found to swing the odds in your favor, use it! The climactic scene of the movie *Rounders*, with Matt Damon, provides a great example of this. Consider professional golfers as well. When someone attempts a long putt, and another player has their ball in proximity, they will walk up near the putt while it's in motion to see how the ball reacts when it approaches the hole.

They want to see how their opponent's ball rolls near the hole so when it's their turn to putt, they have a very good idea how their putt will roll towards the hole. They are taking advantage of observing their opponent's effort to use in their own play on the green.

In your martial arts training, the idea is to observe your instructor very closely. Look for those little nuances in his or her performance that you can try to emulate in your own practice. Make mental notes of the speed, power, pauses, stances, and breathing. What is your instructor doing that allows them to train long, hard, and without seeming to tire out?

Pick up the little details. They didn't become advanced martial artists by accident. Also, observe your instructor's other attributes. How do they conduct themselves both in and out of the dojo? What type of reading material do they have around the house? How do they treat the waiter or waitress at a restaurant?

These may seem trivial or you might make the point that it's my instructor's business regarding those matters and nobody else's business. He or she will live their life, and I'll live mine. I would encourage everyone to extend your concern to a higher level. Observe closely all that is happening around you and, in particular, with your instructor.

What they are teaching you are techniques that can inflict quite a bit of damage to someone, if needed. How your instructor conducts themselves, their interests, and their commitment to being a true martial artist has a direct impact on your learning experiences. What you observe can expand your knowledge, skills, and overall personal development – both regarding martial arts and in life. The potential to use your observation can come from any source. What can you take away from those sources to use in your martial arts? Both of my daughters have been dancers since they were very little. And now my younger daughter is about to begin her college career studying dance at a top ten university in the United States. Her disciplines include ballet, jazz, hip-hop, and modern. She has participated in summer intensive classes with many of the top dancers and choreographers in the dance industry.

After each one, I've discussed with her the experience and what her takeaways were from the program. One example of how observation can pay off came when she attended *Illadelph* in 2019, a dance conference in Philadelphia. She was invited by her hip-hop teachers and attended a session by Rene Harris, who formed the first and longest running hip-hop dance touring company in 1992.

My daughter expressed how much Rene's passion and spirit came through while he was teaching his class. She said, "I could tell he was speaking from the soul. He wanted all of us to understand and feel that passion for hip hop."

According to my daughter, that class helped solidify her goal to pursue a career in the dance profession. What if she hadn't been so observant during that class? What if her mind was elsewhere and she simply was following along and just going through the motions? Fortunately, she was keenly observant that day, which is now paying dividends for her discipline.

A big part of the observation process requires the student to 'feel' the effects of a technique. Walther von Krenner notes this process in his book *Following the Martial Path* where he states, "Originally, martial arts were not taught using detailed explanations. Instead, instructors demonstrated techniques. They expected students to pay attention to what was occurring and then to practice repeatedly until they could duplicate what their instructors had done."

Part of this 'demonstration' was to make the student feel the technique in terms of speed, power, and the specific area of the body being targeted.

This cannot be underestimated in terms of the true learning process. If you don't, on some level, understand the damage a technique can do then it becomes difficult to fully understand the technique, let alone to eventually teach the technique to students who come after you.

It is impossible to fully comprehend and grasp the essence of how a technique works unless you have that face-to-face level of practice. However, learning techniques is the first part and then applying the technique to make it work properly comes next.

With Covid-19 being a major hurdle for gatherings in 2020, many people utilized the Zoom platform to continue their training. Observing how beneficial this platform could be, I used it to work with my instructors in Chi-Ryu Jiujitsu. I would record them performing the CRJ forms on my phone to learn the sequences. Again, this is the first part of any martial art.

Now that restrictions are being lifted across the country, I'll be able to begin the next aspect of learning – applying the technique that I learned over Zoom. This platform now helps everyone where before distance was a hurdle to learning and improving. Keeping in mind the need to eventually get in-person exposure to instruction and the proper learning process for fully absorbing the material, students can deploy sound observation to online training now more than ever.

Observation is one aspect of martial arts
training that is often overlooked.

THE BIBLE OF KARATE | Bubishi

THE BIBLE OF KARATE

KARATE-DŌ

FUNAKOSHI

Eiji Yoshikawa

wabi sabi

EGO IS THE ENEMY

THIS IS
KENDO
ART OF JAPANESE FENCING

"A standard reference work" —Black Belt

Mark Batterson

IN A PIT WITH A LION ON A SNOWY DAY

IN A PIT WITH A LION ON A SNOWY DAY   Batt

ERIK WAHL   THE SPARK AND THE

Olson   Steal My Art   THE LIFE AND TIME T'AI CHI MASTER T.

ARNIS: PRESAS STYLE AND BALISONG

The Writing Warrior   Discovering the Courage to Free Your True Voice

REMAIN A STUDENT

Always be in a position of looking and seeking more knowledge. This requires a consistent effort to ask questions to learn and understand more and more. Keller and Papasan express in their book *The One Thing*, "Answers come from questions, and the quality of any answer is directly determined by the quality of the question. Ask the most powerful question possible, and the answer can be life altering."

This book provides several quotes on questions that really hit home for me: Voltaire stated, "Judge a man by his questions rather than his answers." Gandhi once said, "The power to question is the basis of all human progress." Keller and Papasan write, "Research shows that asking questions improves learning and performance by as much as 150 percent."

It seems as time goes on, we tend to move away from wanting to learn more. This is a massive mistake. I recently watched an interview with Spanish golfer Jon Rahm. This interview was shortly after he won the 2021 U.S. Open.

The interviewer brought up than Jon enjoyed watching old videos of legend Ben Hogan and asked why he does this. Rahm's answer was simply, "You can always learn something." That is the approach to improvement in Rahm's game – remain a student of the game.

This is a key to athletic improvement, but also the key to a fulfilling life in general. However, the easier approach is to settle where we are. This seems to apply to not only new subjects but also within our chosen career paths or the martial arts we practice. It becomes easier to just do things as they've always been done. Apparently, that feels more comfortable, and we'd rather just keep to ourselves and not take a chance at looking foolish with something we don't know about. Take the opposite approach… always remain a student at heart and you'll discover a more fulfilling life.

One of the best ways to remain a student and develop a strong sense of asking questions is to read as much as you can. Becoming an avid reader can expose you to many other aspects of life you might not have otherwise explored. Keller goes on to urge his readers, "uncover the best research and study the highest achievers."

Authors have experiences they want to express in their books. Reading can give you insights into your area of pursuit or into areas that you explore for the first time. Keller explains his purpose for building a personal library, "One of the reasons I've amassed a large library of books over the years is because books are a great go-to resource. Short of having a conversation with someone who has accomplished what you hope to achieve, in my experience books and published works offer the most in terms of documented research and role models for success."

My personal library contains not only martial arts subjects but other diverse topics including works by Christian authors, art, success in business, biographies, Zen philosophy, and sports stories. It is no accident the book you are holding has quotes from all these topics. It is interesting to me how an author on how to become a better writer can provide insights and thoughts that relate to improving the mind within my martial arts training.

Or how a Christian author can bring about thoughts of sound living principles and how to approach goals and aspirations properly knowing that God is the source. Reading a variety of subjects provides expanded thinking and leads to questions and exploration that may not otherwise happen.

I had been a black belt for many, many years when I came across a book titled *Old School – Essays on Japanese Martial Traditions*, by Ellis Amdur. This book documents a style of martial arts using a *kusarigama*, or chain and sickle, called Isshin-Ryu. I had never known another form of martial arts that shared the same name as the system that Grandmaster Tatsuo Shimabuku had formulated in the mid-1950s. Apparently, a samurai of the seventeenth century named Tan Isshin formulated this kusarigama system.

The point: build your personal library. Seek out and research whatever you can regarding the history of not only your current style of karate, but also many other styles of martial arts as well. This process of continuous learning must be a never-ending process to further enhance the value of your training.

There is no stopping point or slowing down with regards to the mentality of remaining a student. This world contains enough opportunities to continually ask questions and learn. When the mind is curious and active, you are truly living.

I have several close friends, fellow martial artists, who lead by example with respect to having a students' mentality. These gentlemen are all over 70 years of age and wish to continue their learning process. They aren't wasting their time doing the same old things.

John Costanzo was a web designer and programmer for AT&T and retired as a computer science teacher. However, he recently stepped out of his comfort zone and started exploring photoshop. He has found a new path to enrich his knowledge and skills. Look at the cover of the book you're holding, and you'll notice the fruits of John's pursuit of remaining a student.

John McDonald is an accomplished actor and writer and co-wrote the screenplay for the movie *By the Sword*, released in 1991, starring F. Murray Abraham and Eric Roberts. Not resting on this success, John went on to become director of operations for Carnegie Hall. Now, John is a monologue coach for high school seniors preparing for their college auditions.

He instructs and mentors high school students looking to get into major universities for their performing arts programs. He kept his focus on continually learning and his acting students have a very high acceptance rate to college.

And Isham Latimer applies his martial arts background and knowledge to instructing law enforcement for the New York State Division of Parole.

All three of these men lead by example, they 'remain a student' as success is simply a point in time to catch your breath, reassess where you are and your goals, and then move onward to more growth.

Keeping thoughts of always being a student should go with you everywhere. When I took my daughters on a trip to Spain in 2019 (they were 19 and 16 at the time) to visit with their grandfather (on their mother's side) I told them to ask a lot of questions. They were lucky to have their grandfather serve as tour guide, so to speak, and this opportunity was perfect to expand their horizons and learn about another culture.

They followed the advice and came away with priceless experiences and memories which, using the mentality of always trying to learn new things, they can adopt in all their travels to new destinations. Simply put, remaining a student is a mindset that can make life much richer and fun to live.

KEEP EXPLORING

One of the most damaging things to our purpose in life is to settle where we are, to get comfortable after achieving a certain level of success. We need to develop a mindset and work ethic to continually explore the possibilities that are out there. A quote by one of my favorite authors, Mitch Albom, makes a great point, "What we carry defines who we are. And the effort we make is our legacy." Anyone can settle where they are; it's not difficult. Those who continually push themselves and explore all that is around them to improve and grow will reap the benefits of this effort. Those who explore will be the people everyone talks about.

Exploration requires you to try new things and see where improvements can be made. No matter what it is you are doing, having a desire to explore new paths creates questions leading to answers that would have never been sought in the first place.

A good friend came upon a quote by comedian George Carlin that expresses this need for exploration: "Doing new stuff is a point of pride with me. People may not consider it so, but stand-up comedy is one of the performing arts, and artists are supposed to grow and evolve over time. Through the years, my technique has sharpened, my writing has improved and even my observations have grown richer. I can't do old material;

I would feel like a failure. Essentially, this job is that of a writer, but a writer who doesn't produce new work all the time is not a writer – he's a typist."

George Carlin clearly understood that resting upon a bit of success will lead to complacency and stagnation. Always doing "old material" doesn't lead to growth. This same philosophy applies to everything you do.

Author Laraine Herring puts it this way in her book *The Writing Warrior*, "Be an active participant in your learning and be open [explore] to all that's around you." This thought applies to everything you do, and not just learning to be a better writer.

In the martial arts, the sensei provides the framework for the student to learn the art. But the student is in full control of their progress. This progress can become much more meaningful and rounded if the student keeps an open mind and looks for learning opportunities everywhere, both inside or outside of the dojo from both a physical and mental perspective. This is often referred to as *shoshin*, which means 'beginner mind.'

You must continually have the mindset of a beginner. Never fall into the trap of thinking you've arrived after reaching a specific goal or rank level. When you continually think using a beginner's mindset, your mind remains open to new ideas, and exploring new things then becomes a habit. You remain diligent in trying new paths to determine the best approach to progress.

With my traditional Shodo art, I'm continually trying different things. I work with acrylic paints and pastels and try different colors and combinations. I want to see how people react to the results. My idea is not to be concerned with being precise or perfect as we all know perfection is not reality. Relax and enjoy the process of exploring new things.

At a conference for work, the sponsors had artist Erik Wahl perform. Wahl is a painter using a modern style called 'speed painting.' His presentation held my full attention considering my interest in painting. At one point he mentioned children are such good creators because they are not concerned with how their art will turn out. As adults we become too self-conscious. We are afraid of failing or looking like a fool. We stop exploring the same way we did when we were younger.

Failure is one of life's best learning tools, if not the best for many people. One of the best ways of facing and overcoming failure is being exposed to failure in small doses. When you stumble in your martial arts training or have a small setback it can show you it's not the end of the world.

Recognize the small failure for what it is, an experience to help you continue to improve and maintain a focused attitude. Keep exploring, keep looking at whatever you're doing from all angles. Pay close attention to others and see if there's something you can garner from what they are doing. Explore other arts. The movements from their systems could possibly enhance what you currently do.

The other part of the 'failure' equation is that maybe you just weren't ready for that promotion, or the next rank in your martial art, or public's acceptance and appreciation of your writing or your artwork. Messing up something and not being quite ready for the next level are both a type of failure, but they are not the same.

Chances are likely very high that you simply weren't quite ready for the success. Keep exploring. Keep pushing forward as the breakthrough is one day closer than you realize. You cannot find success without first risking failure. Unless you're willing to fail on both a small and large scale, then success will be hard to find. Only hard work with stumbles along the way to produce improvement that is hard-won and worth the effort.

◆

You must continually have the mindset of a beginner.

GROWTH COMES FROM WITHIN

Real personal growth, whatever the endeavor, can only come about when your view of yourself is positive. Reflective thoughts from time-to-time on what you're doing and what are your purpose and goals is a key element to your growth. How do you feel about yourself and the path you are currently following? Notice I didn't say how do you feel compared to others.

The second we begin comparing ourselves with others, we lose focus on what really matters. Just the same as we are all different, so too is our purpose and the rate of growth we develop. We cannot possibly be on the same path as another. Therefore, others can only help or motivate us along the way. We are all responsible for our own growth, and that begins with a positive framework.

To have positive thoughts about yourself and your progress, you need to work on clearing out the negativity that invariably creeps into your thinking.

Author Mark Batterson makes the point of "unlearning" in his book *In a Pit With a Lion on a Snowy Day* where he explains, "Almost like a hard drive with a computer virus, our minds have infected files. Irrational fears and misconceptions keep us from operating the way we were designed to. And if those fears and misconceptions aren't uninstalled, they undermine everything we do."

As Batterson notes, it is much more difficult to unlearn negative thoughts and behaviors than it is to learn new things and bring in new information. This can only happen when we consciously think positively about ourselves and avoid the temptation to compare ourselves and our progress with others.

Comparisons are a complete waste of your time and energy. While you're trying to measure up and compare yourself with others, you cannot possibly focus on the things that can help you move forward and grow. The path they are on, and their rate of growth and achievement are not yours. Focus on you and what you can control.

With your martial arts training, do not wait for others to help you in your personal growth and development. Growth must come from within you. Do not expect others to travel the path with you, or to help you at every step along the way. If you think your training is only within the walls of the dojo or require others to travel with you to training sessions or seminars, your growth will surely have a very low ceiling as invariably nobody else is on the same schedule as you.

Your martial arts training should be a vehicle to learn more about yourself, to solve problems thus leading to personal growth. If you are able to take initiative of your own training and learning how to solve your own problems or the hurdles that you face, then you are well on your way to inner growth as a martial artist and as a person.

Sensei Steven Ballenger states in his book *Shorin-Ryu Karatedo – Temple of the Young Trees*, "From the beginning of the point which the student becomes dedicated to the art, the practice of karate-do is a physiological, psychological, sociological and philosophical progression of continuous growth."

Sensei Ballenger then goes on to explain a higher level of purpose in karate training stating, "It is your own problems you solve. Karate exposes the error of your ways. Karate-do is but a branch in the 'tree of life' which cannot grow until the person who follows it gives it root and the spirit life."

There is a major benefit to your training in that you learn how to adapt, grow, change, and solve your own problems through consistent and dedicated practice. These changes must come from within. Your sensei cannot force those changes to occur. Your fellow students cannot enable or trigger those changes to take place. They can only come from within you.

Others can assist, guide, listen, and make suggestions from their own experiences and learned knowledge. But true growth cannot happen unless you set your mind to it and take the initiative – travel and work with others, practice on your own, make the time to train, make it fit your schedule, and don't wait for the next class to research and explore.

Let's face the truth: if you need your hand held in whatever endeavor you pursue – martial arts or otherwise – you're not training, instead you're simply participating in a physical activity. There is a big difference between the two.

Some may turn to or consider meditation to keep a steady stream of positive thoughts. What works for everyone is different. But the bottom line is consistency, ongoing activity of some type to ensure growth from within is happening. This 'growth' is due in large part to expanded brain development due to this consistent activity whether it's exercise, research in topics of interest, writing, painting, or martial arts.

Batterson points out a study by doctors Avi Karni and Leslie Ungerleider of the National Institute of Mental Health. They asked subjects to perform a simple motor task – a finger-tapping exercise. They conducted an MRI scan on the subjects during the exercise to determine what part of the brain was activated. After four weeks of consistent practice of this finger-tapping motion, the subjects were re-scanned, and the doctors discovered the brain activity in the same area had expanded. This simple task "literally recruited new nerve cells and rewired neuronal connections." These results show that consistency is the key for development of 'growth from within.'

REPETITION

The key to improvement and proficiency, regardless of the activity, is repetition. Being able to successfully repeat a motion or action, whether it's within a sport or some type of artistic endeavor, is the key element to take yourself to higher levels. When you see someone with a high degree of skill, you need to realize that what got them to that point was tireless repetition.

Authors Gary Keller and Jay Papasan explain in their book *The One Thing*, "At some point white belts training to advance know the same basic karate moves black belts know – they simply haven't practiced enough to be able to do them as well. The creativity you see at a black belt level comes from mastery of the white belt fundamentals."

The sticking point for many though is overcoming the boredom associated with repetition. For example, while running on the treadmill one of the tricks I use to stave off the boredom is focusing on my running form and technique. Taking note of my stride length, breathing, whether my hands are tensed into fists and draining my energy – all of these are recurring thoughts instead of the dread of the repetition involved.

Performing in a consistent, efficient manner on the treadmill can remove the boredom and keep your mind so focused that the run is completed before you know it.

Whether you cover a mile or a marathon, a focused mind on the execution of consistent movement will put your mind at ease regarding the extent of the activity.

Take notice of a baseball pitcher in the midst of throwing a no-hitter. Watch his movements on the mound and you'll likely notice he is repeating the same exact motions every time, without fail. He knows he must repeat every nuance of his activity in the same exact way. This is because he knows repetition leads to not only efficiency, but also keeping his mind off the overwhelming thought of what he is trying to do.

The same holds true for golfers. If you cannot repeat the swing effectively, you will fail miserably time and time again. This can only be accomplished through grueling repetition. In fact, you should have the attitude of thoroughly enjoying the repetitive nature of practice.

This is what led Ben Hogan to become one of the greatest golfers in history. In his prime in the 1950s, he was once interrupted during a three-hour practice session that had begun only minutes after he had shot a tournament-leading round of 66. Hogan said to the interviewer: "When I'm not playing, I like to be practicing. I enjoy every minute of playing and practicing. To tell you the truth, I'd just as soon do this."

The concept of repetition also applies to martial arts training. First, the student should develop a clear vision on what his or her goal is. From there, a plan is crafted to train diligently to meet the goal. The preparation must be relentless and to the point where the student can 'see' the goal being met.

David Chadwick notes in his book *It's How You Play the Game*, "Preparation exacerbates the power of positive words in pressure situations."

When the student finds a good instructor, who imparts ongoing words of encouragement, and then couples that with relentless preparation, the results are definitive and sound. This in turn yields confidence that can help the student not only in their martial arts training but all throughout the challenges that life can throw at them.

Laraine Herring in her book *The Writing Warrior* notes this about the profession of being a writer, "Writing is both flow and discipline. Art and craft. Intuition and perspiration." If you didn't know the source of the quote, the experienced martial artist would think its topic was about martial arts. The parallels are very interesting.

What Herring is pointing out regarding the career of writing is that you must write every day. You must discipline yourself to stay involved in the practice of writing whether the process is flowing naturally, or you are struggling for whatever reason. Repetitive actions lead to improvement.

The same can be said about any endeavor to which the practitioner takes seriously. My late Kendo sensei, Duk Yeong Kim, would often tell me to practice my sword cuts five thousand times every day. Back then I thought to myself, "Is he serious?!" Years later, I realize that he was. If you truly wish to improve and become proficient, you must carve out the time it takes to perform those five thousand repetitive cutting motions without fail.

Think this repetition thing is just a mindset? There's math behind the concept to validate it. Keller and Papasan disclose in *The One Thing* a published journal in the *Psychological Review* about the benchmark for mastery.

The journal's author K. Anders Ericsson discloses his findings on the 10,000-hour rule. They state, "His research identified a common pattern of regular and deliberate practice over the course of years in elite performers that made them what they were – elite...Many elite performers complete their journey in about ten years."

The need, and subsequent value, of repetition in whatever area you choose to pursue cannot be understated. It is a cornerstone of any potential success you are pursuing.

Training in martial arts requires you to go outside of your comfort zone. This is summarized extremely well in the book *Following the Martial Path,* by Walther von Krenner, where he writes, "Real training is difficult. It takes constant effort. It requires self-reflection and a selfless approach to training. One must train with no thought whatsoever of pain and suffering. Students have to push themselves to rise above such distractors."

If you can learn the power of repetition and achieve a goal, then the level of repetition used to achieve that goal can be used to improve other facets of your life. You can take the experience from meeting various goals and apply it to anything else – martial arts practice, weight training, education, a promotion for your job, etc.

There needs to be an ongoing routine in your training. Herring refers to the concept of "unconscious competence" when discussing routines and becoming a better writer. When you have an ongoing, dedicated routine to whatever you are doing – writing, running, swimming, art, your work, martial arts – then you will improve often times at a pace that you may not even be aware of.

Competence creeps into your activity almost in an unconscious manner. Then as you learn new things along the way, your 'routine' or your 'repetition' will reinforce what was learned to the point that it will be retained in long-term memory. This is the key to the structure of martial arts training – consistent, repetitive practice leads to success.

PERSEVERANCE

Everyone must deal with setbacks, problems, and disappointments. These are inevitably a part of life. They may be extremely painful and upsetting, but they are also one of the keys to your growth. As Max Lucado writes in his book *More to Your Story*, "Times of testing are actually times of training, purification, and strength building."

Overcoming the pitfalls of life will help you to persevere when you need it most. Lucado further instructs, "You can even 'consider it pure joy...whenever you face trials of many kinds, because you know that the testing of your faith produces perseverance.'" (James 1:2 – 3)

Consistency and daily habits become essential to develop and solidify your perseverance. Whatever it is that you pursue to improve yourself and your skills, you must make it a part of your everyday life. When you can focus on those daily habits, the failures and setbacks seem to fade. Your mind becomes so in tune with what you need to do to work on your skills that slowly, but surely, success follows.

Ceaseless daily practice, or *heiso ni ari*, is explained in *Zen Word, Zen Calligraphy* where author Eido Tai Shimano writes, "When days pass without any problems, the results of the accumulation of such practice may not be revealed so drastically, but when unexpected, extraordinary things happen, one's everyday practice and everyday mindfulness arise spontaneously and accordingly. Since life, in general, is unpredictable, we need to prepare to meet these unpredictable happenings. Hence, it is extremely important for us to continue daily practice."

Therefore, when bad things happen to you it is critical to dive back into your practices: art, writing, sports, martial arts, school studies. Certainly, a period of grieving or reflection is necessary. We are only human. But getting back into your daily practice routine is paramount to maintaining your perseverance to overcome that setback and move forward. Those training habits are a part of who you are in the first place. And they are needed to get you back on track to remaining who you were meant to be and eventually become.

I personally have had a couple of big setbacks over the past 15 years. Each time, I turned back to my prayer life and my martial arts training to pull me through. I was able to persevere and improve in my martial arts as my daily habits included my training. My mind could focus on improving my skills instead of worrying about the pain.

Most recently, I was able to cross over into more artistic endeavors such as authoring books and exploring different painting styles. These areas were always a point of interest for me but going through difficulties and suffering provided the spark to give them a formal attempt. I knew that to persevere I had to develop positive habits.

Authors Keller and Papasan explain in their book *The One Thing*, "Success is not a marathon of disciplined action. Success is actually a short race – a sprint fueled by discipline just long enough for habit to kick in and take over."

Perseverance takes tremendous effort, for sure. But the key is small steps. First, develop a positive habit through a short burst of discipline, which leads to consistency in daily life, and ultimately leads you to persevere and overcome.

According to Keller and Papasan, "When you discipline yourself, you're essentially training yourself to act in a specific way. Stay with this long enough and it becomes routine – in other words, a habit."

These authors disclose in their book that a University College of London study revealed it takes an average of 66 days to acquire a new habit. Additional studies also reveal that positive habits are beneficial in many other ways including less stress, lower compulsive spending, and more nutritional eating.

Of course, having the discipline to develop habits requires you to completely love what it is you are practicing. When your mind is at the point where you love to practice a specific sport or a particular activity, then self-discipline to work on those things every day becomes second nature. You don't have to think about it. In fact, when you happen to miss a day of practice then something doesn't feel right.

After my setbacks when I finally got back into my martial arts practice, I loved working on the various arts

I practiced. It was something that brought joy back into my life. Successful athletes, artists, musicians, and entrepreneurs will tell you how much they love working on their craft. It is a part of who they are.

In my competitive days as a martial artist, losing didn't affect me for very long. Everyone would rather win than lose, but I took the loss as an opportunity to go back and figure out how to improve my performance. I knew I had to adjust some things and develop better habits in my practice.

I didn't mind this process. I loved it. I looked forward to every workout to determine how to better my skills. I wanted to persevere in my attempts to fare better at the next competition. The pain of all the losses was short-lived. The perseverance I gained from overcoming those losses paid dividends not only in martial arts, but in my personal life as well.

ANGER

I'm a big fan of books written by Max Lucado. This author, in my opinion, has the ability to take concepts and passages from the Bible and put them into plain language. He takes the stories of the Bible and the life of Jesus Christ and relates them to current day news and experiences. His book titled *He Chose the Nails* touches upon the topic of anger.

We all show our dark side now and then. It's inevitable because we all have this propensity to get angry, which leads to hurting others – intentionally or unintentionally. There's no way around it, and we cannot completely remove this from our spirit. This is similar to hate. I've heard people say, "I hate this person or that person." Or "I hate it when he or she does…"

When my daughters make statements such as these, I remind them that the word hate (anger) has such a finality to it, and that God would rather for us to avoid such people or, better yet, improve ourselves to avoid such hate and anger.

Lucado brings up the point to reflect on our own experiences. Have you ever: Cut off someone in traffic? Flashed your high beams on the car in front of you who is going too slow? Made fun of a co-worker or politician on your social media account? Exploded on your kids for something insignificant because of stress going on with work or a friend?

Regardless of the degree of the reaction, it's all classified as anger. All these examples, and many others I'm sure you can recall, leads to nothing of value. This is very much the current state of our politics, the media, and social media used heavily today. Nothing is getting done for the overall good and people are only getting more divided.

The ability to suppress anger and hate is of paramount importance, especially today.

In his book *Moving Toward Stillness*, author Dave Lowry tells the story of a samurai warrior who had mastered this ability. There was battle taking place for sixteenth century Japan between Takeda Shingen and Uyesugi Kenshin. At one point, Kenshin grew impatient and angry at the pace of the battle and invaded Shingen's camp. He drew his sword and held it over Shingen ready to strike. Shingen, sitting there totally calm, gently tapped Kenshin's sword stating, "A flake of snow on a blazing stove."

Impressed by Shingen's ability to control his emotions, Kenshin returned his sword and rode away on horseback. In essence, Shingen was proving the point that in anger you will act out of character and lack any sense of control. Anger will lead to nothing but problems and, most likely, a domino effect of negative outcomes.

This is something every martial artist must come to terms with and develop in their training. You should always be in tune with your emotions and when anger is beginning to take root, learn to deal with it and suppress it so you can react calmly and naturally.

I see people on social media post angry and hateful messages, all the time. This includes martial artists who I've never met, but ones who I respect as I've read their books and magazine articles, which have proven helpful and motivational in my own training. Nobody seems immune, as we are all simply human. But why would anyone, let alone some very well-known authors of the martial arts, post on social media to degrade another artist or prove to be hateful or angry to someone?

If you have a solid background and have been blessed with great instructors over the years, what could possibly be the point in those posts? What is gained by expressing hate or anger to others on social media? It's certainly a disappointing showing of those people. Avoiding this type of behavior or having the ability to control that anger, although much more difficult to do, is clearly the better way to go, even when the anger is initially directed towards you.

When people show anger, there is something clearly out of sorts in that person's life. Anger festers and grows until something bad or unfortunate happens. At this point it's too late.

I've heard my karate sensei say, "You can cover up a hole in a piece of wood put there by a nail, but the hole will always remain." Both of my daughters work for a local boutique. Sometimes customers come into the store, and they are angry. So much so that they lash out in anger with profanity and yelling. All the customer sees is a teenager behind the counter who is trying to follow store policy and the customer's issue, whatever it is, cannot be handled to their satisfaction.

My girls have come home in tears on occasion. I try to tell them it's not anything they did to set off the customer. They have something wrong going on in their life and they need someone to dump their issues on, someone to vent their anger onto. Don't accept the baggage they offer. Take the high road and suppress your own anger. Others will notice what you're doing and benefit from your example. And that could very well snowball into a better way of life for yourself and everyone around you. As author Max Lucado says, "How we treat others is how we treat Jesus."

RESEARCH

When you continually research and explore your interests, God seems to always give you a boost or a lift when you need it. Sometimes, even in unexpected ways from unrelated issues.

I read a variety of books on various topics ranging from martial arts to autobiographies to sports to religion. From time-to-time, a thought or a feeling jumps out from reading books that I can apply to my own writings.

Mark Batterson makes this point as well in his book *In a Pit With a Lion on a Snowy Day* where he writes, "When I read a good book, the Holy Spirit has a way of surfacing thoughts and feelings that have lain dormant for months or years. Sometimes a forgotten dream surfaces. Or an unresolved problem. Or an unnoticed opportunity."

The concept is simple: put yourself in the mode of researching or learning, whether on the topic of your interest or just a leisure activity. The trick is staying in that mode as much as possible. That is a fundamental purpose of our lives, continuing to learn and improve.

You cannot learn and advance without engaging in activities that require some level of effort such as reading, trying new activities or exercises, listening to others within your field, etc. We tend to want to break now and then from whatever it is we are working on or pursuing. This is normal and often is needed for our sanity.

But even during those 'down times' keep your mind open and aware. Pay attention to the little things as this may lead to new ideas. The famous swordsman Miyamoto Musashi is said to have developed his two-sword system by watching a taiko drummer. He figured holding a sword in both hands would expand the possibilities of his own techniques, which history shows us was a correct assessment.

You need to get yourself out of your comfort zone. Try new things. Read different books. Batterson goes on to state, "If you want God to do something new, you can't keep doing the same old thing. What got you here won't automatically get you where God wants you to go next."

You need not worry specifically where or how you'll get there. Just keep working and researching to expand your knowledge and exposure to many other things. The right doors will open at the right time.

Everyone in life we encounter or cross paths with can help us along on our journey. Some help a little, some a lot. It's all worth it. It doesn't matter who, or what, they help us with. They help to propel us along the path to being a better martial artist and hopefully, a better person.

Therefore, keep looking all around for research and experience opportunities. In your martial arts training, continue going to competitions or tournaments. They have a great level of value whether you compete or assist with judging competitors. Research leads to figuring out how to improve and succeed in your chosen field.

Students must be willing to put in the time and effort to learn as much as possible about their chosen art. At a certain point in time, they will logically wish to extend that knowledge outside of their main system and begin looking into other arts as well.

Not knowing is bad, but not wishing to know is much worse and detrimental to the development as a martial artist and as an individual. This may sound like a simple truth, but many people often fall into learning traps where they reach a certain level and then have no further desire to expand their knowledge base. There is so much history in martial arts. The student, regardless of age or rank, should have a never-ending aspiration to learn as much history on the martial arts as possible.

Studying other martial arts provides you an expanded perspective on your training and research into not only your respective style but also other systems. You will quickly learn that your style isn't the only one that has all the answers for self-defense. Keep in mind that every system is an expression of the techniques and movements that worked well for the founder of each respective style.

Not every style is meant to work well for everyone; however, you can garner insights and pick up specific movements and techniques if you look around and research other systems and styles of martial arts. There is an entire universe of martial arts that offer much to those willing to open their minds and learn.

The key here is to remain open to all forms of martial arts instead of having closed-minded thinking. However, a martial artist seeks as much knowledge as possible to blend with their core system. Using Isshin-Ryu karate as an example, which is a combination of two major branches of Okinawan martial arts: Shorin-Ryu and Goju-Ryu. The founder took specific kata and training concepts from both systems.

What about those kata which he didn't pull into his Isshin-Ryu system? Having an interest to learn and research those other kata can provide you a perspective that would never develop if you only focus on the kata contained within the Isshin-Ryu curriculum.

My training in Filipino martial arts is under the organization SMP Arnis. Within that organization, we include training and research into several styles such as Modern Arnis, Kombatan, Balintawak, and Serrada Escrima. It is important to cross over and experience other styles and to research the backgrounds and techniques of others to grow as an artist.

What's interesting based upon my own research is that many of the leading martial artists also seek out other styles and continually research as well. It is quite common for practitioners of Japanese-based systems to train in Chinese or Filipino martial arts and vice versa. Your own research will undoubtedly uncover this fact repeatedly.

In the book *The Writing Warrior*, Laraine Herring writes, "While theory can help you find new ways of looking at problems and activities, and help you think more critically about your own choices and reactions, what matters most is your direct experience…"

In other words, if you only practice and research one style or method of training, you will tend to only reflect those teachings in your performance, and your growth will be limited. Go outside of your normal routines and study other arts. If you are passionate and serious, then your craft should never be limited to your genre.

YOUR SENSEI'S APPROACH

Everything in martial arts begins with and is built upon the relationship between the sensei and the student. There is nothing more important to your overall development as a lifelong student of the martial arts.

It is often stated that you can tell who the instructor is by how the student conducts themselves. This concept has merit both within the dojo and how the student is perceived in their public life. You want to find an instructor that you want to emulate and follow.

When people ask me about finding a good instructor or martial arts school, I always tell them to be patient and look around. Take your time to find a place where you feel the sensei, or teacher, has not only good skills but leaves a positive impression on you. Before deciding upon a style and sensei to train with, remember that martial arts training is meant to be a lifetime journey.

The sensei should not only teach you self-defense and the history of the art they are teaching, he or she should be of good character – both within the dojo and in everyday life. The sensei is not a parent by any means. But on the other hand, having a sensei that sets good examples, is diligent in their training and goal setting, treats everyone with respect and courtesy, and is continually challenging himself or herself and never wants their learning to end – those types of teachers can teach you more than you realize outside of the dojo as well.

During your training, take note and try to figure out your sensei's approach to training and learning. Leave behind prior training methods and thought processes and work to mirror his or her approach to their art.

This isn't necessarily a physical thing. Observe and discuss the arts with your sensei. Time and patience are essential as this will be needed to pull out of your sensei those essential thoughts and ideas that you can apply to your own approach to training and learning.

My Isshin-Ryu karate sensei, Grandmaster Toby Cooling, has always stated, "Teach everything you know, and the knowledge will come back to you double." This has stuck with me over the years, and I try to follow this principle when teaching my students or leading a seminar.

Freely sharing your knowledge has a way of paying you back. You eventually find yourself working and training with others having more knowledge since the goal is to never stop learning yourself. It's a never-ending cycle that can reward you time and time again when you teach all that you know.

Sitting down and discussing life on a variety of topics is an essential part of understanding your martial art, albeit on an indirect level. I feel this is a quality of Isshin-Ryu (one heart) karate.

What lies at the core of your sensei's heart? This is a concept that is not always spoken, but one that is essential to uncover if your training will have any sort of meaning. How can anyone think they can garner the deeper instruction of their instructor unless they can truly understand and respect the person on an intellectual and emotional level?

Your sensei is not perfect. Your sensei, man or woman, has strengths and weaknesses both within your chosen martial art as well as in their personal life. Get to know them, for everything that they are and have been through can teach you something about yourself.

I have traveled to Nevada many times to visit Grandmaster Cooling at his home. I would estimate that 80 percent of the time spent with my sensei has nothing to do with martial arts technique. This is by design. You need to come to some level of trust with your instructors, and they in turn need to come to that same level with you.

They are passing down an art to which they have devoted their entire life. The lessons they learned both in and out of the dojo in their experiences are invaluable. You cannot put a price tag on what they possess and how much those lessons, learned and cultivated from seriously hard work, can help you in your own martial arts training and in the obstacles that you face in everyday life.

It takes an immense amount of time and effort to pass down the martial arts in the intended manner. If you rely on this transmission of the art only within the walls of the dojo, you are missing at least half of the overall picture.

Martial arts are not a pursuit to be taken lightly. Serious damage can be inflicted not only to others, but also to yourself if you do not learn and practice responsibly. This can also extend to damage of your instructor's reputation as well as the organization to which you belong.

As such, good instructors do not freely give away all their knowledge – nor should they – just because you pay a monthly fee to train within their dojo. The sensei needs to have a very high degree of confidence that you will respect and preserve their teachings and not damage everything they've trained so hard to attain before ever meeting you, the student.

This takes time. This takes an effort on your part beyond simply showing up and training with many others at the same time. You don't want to be just another number in the dojo. You should seek out personal transmission of the sensei's art. You need to get to know your sensei beyond the walls of the dojo – on many levels.

Developing as strong a bond as possible with your sensei can be a life-changing experience. It is no different with a coach, a teacher, a friend, or a distant relative. When developed correctly, this mentorship experience can and will last a lifetime. A good sensei will realize that this relationship will be as beneficial to them as it is to the student. When the sensei can see the student's heart better, when the sensei knows the dedication of the student is true, he will be apt to share more information as well as the sensei's well-earned experiences to further improve the student.

EXCUSES

Excuses are the easiest thing in the world. Coming up with some type of reason why you didn't accomplish a goal, or why you didn't get something done, or why you didn't show up to an event of some sort doesn't require an instruction manual or guidebook. It seems everyone knows automatically how to make excuses from very little and well into adulthood.

I got my Bachelor of Science degree in accounting and had a goal of passing the CPA exam shortly thereafter. At the time, the exam consisted of four parts: auditing, business law, accounting and reporting, and financial accounting and reporting. On my first attempt in taking the exam, I passed auditing and business law as they were my favorite classes in college. I earned credit for those two parts and wouldn't need to re-take those sections of the exam.

According to the AICPA, I had five years to pass the other two sections. Considering that tax, financial accounting, and cost accounting were subjects I struggled with, the excuses started to emerge. *This new job takes up a lot of my time. I'll study harder for the next exam. My classes were part-time in school, so I can't remember what I learned in that tax course anymore.* It was easier to come up with all sorts of excuses for not buckling down and studying harder to pass the remaining sections of the exam.

Eventually, my conditional credit for passing auditing and business law expired, and the CPA was now in the rearview mirror. Essentially, I talked myself out of passing the CPA because it was easier to make excuses than it was to commit everything I had into my goal.

After delving into a new career as an IT auditor, I set a goal of earning the credential of a Certified Information Systems Auditor, or CISA. This time, my mind was convinced I was not going to repeat the mistakes made with the CPA exam. My mind was set that I was going to reach this goal. I was prepared to put in the time to study and drill the practice questions with everything I had.

I set a schedule for myself to follow for my preparation and I made sure I stuck to the plan. I wasn't about to allow excuses to creep into my thinking this time. The change paid off and I earned the CISA credential on my first attempt at the exam. Excuses are the enemy to your progress and growth. Your mind is what is needed to control them.

Don't provide excuses when it comes to your martial arts training or any other endeavor that you take seriously. If you have a goal in mind, work relentlessly until the goal is reached. If you fall short or something or someone is hindering the result you're looking for, don't provide excuses.

For example, if you train and prepare for a karate tournament and the judges score your performance below your expectation, don't begin to make excuses such as, "Well, they don't really know me or my style of karate so they don't really have a sound basis on which to score me."

You're focusing on the wrong things. You should be reflecting on those who did well and placed higher than you. What made them stand out? Is there something you can take away from the experience and begin to work on for the next tournament? If you lean on this or that excuse, then your original goal probably didn't mean that much to you in the first place.

The mind is the essential piece to the puzzle of success. You must believe in yourself and your goal with every ounce of your being. If this is not in place, then the excuses will surely come as people believe excuses justify falling short.

Norman Vincent Peale makes this point in his book *The Power of Positive Thinking*, "People are defeated in life not because of lack of ability, but for lack of wholeheartedness. They do not wholeheartedly expect to succeed. Their heart isn't in it, which is to say themselves are not fully given. Results do not yield themselves to the person who refuses to give himself to the desired results."

This is exactly why I didn't succeed in passing the CPA exam. I justified my excuses because I didn't commit fully to the process. Even though I took classes parttime throughout school and felt the material wasn't fresh, I still had the ability to succeed. However, the excuses won out.

Peale goes on to explain how putting your entire heart into something is how to keep excuses at bay. He says, "Heart is the symbol of creative activity. Fire the heart with where you want to go and what you want to be... your entire personality will follow where your heart leads."

Since I didn't wholeheartedly put myself into passing the CPA exam, there was no way I was going to get where I wanted to go.

Peale also makes the point that our attitudes toward our obstacles or difficulties are mental. He explains, "What you think about your obstacles largely determines what you do about them."

In other words, whether you think something cannot be done or believe you can overcome a hurdle or obstacle – in both situations the result tends to follow your mental attitude. Without fail, excuses will feed your doubt. The objective is to recognize the excuses and eliminate them by wholeheartedly approaching your goal.

Excuses can formulate from a mindset that is not fully committed, as noted previously. They can also stem from a fear of failure or looking bad at trying something new. However, if your perspective is in the right place then failure can serve you incredibly well by being a learning mechanism.

Many athletes who have succeeded in their sport often cite the number of times they've failed. They know that failure is a part of the process for their respective sport. The same is true for your martial arts training. Failures can add to your abilities by learning from them. A failure or setback provides the opportunity to learn, to look inward and seek what went wrong. Only then can you appreciate the efforts you put forth, to be proud of your commitment to your craft.

Failures not only develop your physical abilities but also your patience and your mental toughness. Using the example of karate competition earlier, it took me many attempts to finally find myself in the top three in competition when I was starting out in karate.

It was frustrating not seeing any results from my practice in getting ready for those competitions. I'd put in extra hours on my kata, or forms, performance only to see others do better than me. But I also understood that it wasn't necessarily failure but rather I wasn't hitting the proper marks that others were able to do.

I made it a point to use my so-called 'failure' to my advantage. I watched all the competitors very closely and noted the scores they received. I made mental notes on their abilities and performances and took that home to replay over and over in my mind to then try and apply what they were doing.

There was no time for excuses. I had goals in mind and used my failed past experiences to fuel my motivation to work harder and smarter. I could have easily justified those failures with excuses. Rather, I flipped the script and told myself *you're not quite there yet. But soon you will be*. Viewing failure as a critical component of your training can lead to your eventual improvement as a martial artist. Excuses will defeat you only if you allow them to.

OTHERS

"The martial way of life practiced by warriors is based on excelling others in anything and everything." This quote from the famous swordsman Miyamoto Musashi is documented in his writings titled *The Book of Five Rings*, written in 1643.

Helping others on their path or journey is certainly a rewarding experience. Examples would include setting up a contact for someone to get an interview for a job or writing a letter of recommendation for someone to a college or future employer.

Other ways to help others would be giving mentoring advice to a family friend or reviewing a work product for a co-worker before submission. These are examples of 'excelling others' which are relevant in today's society.

Musashi ties this concept to the martial way of life. This is an interesting point that must always be an integral part of every modern martial artist's awareness and consideration.

We should consciously work to integrate a concern for others and help them in any way we can to improve and assist them along in their journey. You never know when your efforts will double back to you and those who you helped. They could very well help you in your time of need.

Hurting people is easy, especially when they do something negative towards you. God taught his followers to turn the other cheek. This is crucial to keep your mind going in the right direction, which should be to continually improve yourself.

If you constantly think about how someone's done you wrong and how you will re-pay them, that will only cause more damage to yourself both mentally and emotionally. Any effort to undermine someone else rather than helping others is a complete waste of your time and energy. And studies have shown these areas, if affected over a period time, will only cause damage to you physically as well.

Max Lucado writes in his book *Jesus – The God Who Knows Your Name*, "Are not our bodies holy? Our tongues, our hands, our brains are the dwelling place and tools of God. Yet when I use this tongue to hurt, these hands to injure, this brain for my glory and not God's, am I not vandalizing God's temple?"

If you are hurting others, you are not serving the purpose for which God provided the tools and gifts you possess. As martial artists, we should be the example of hard work, perseverance, goal setting, and lifting others to higher levels of performance and achievement.

The karate family to which I belong, the Order of Isshin-Ryu Martial Arts, has a code of ethics documented for all to follow. The very first one states, "A karate-ka is fierce in battle, and gentle in life."

This code is attributed to Sensei Malachi Lee. One who is a martial artist must set a strong example and be not only a leader of the technical skills required of the arts, but also a leader in how you treat others and how you help them whenever possible.

The world has enough negativity already, and social media is not helping in any way. When you make fun of others or talk about others to demean them or try to trip them up, what is the point? What is gained in the process of trying to humiliate or talk about other people?

Yet people continue to do so all the time. You see this in politics and in the media constantly. There is always some angle or some personal agenda that everyone seems to be pushing to make others look badly so you can get ahead.

Just focus on continually improving yourself. Believe it or not, this will have an impact on the naysayers in your life. They will notice their words are not taking effect and likely will move on to someone else. And from time-to-time, they will take note of your resolve to better yourself and others and may even end up wanting you to help teach them to improve.

I watched in interview once on Major League Baseball Network by Bob Costas. He was discussing records with the legendary Hank Aaron. Costas asked him about all the records he attained in his career and the impressions Aaron had of the game of baseball leading up to his place in the Hall of Fame.

Aaron responded interestingly by saying, "I never concerned myself about the baseball side of things. I was always wondering if, after baseball, could I make a difference. Could I do something of value and leave an impact on others and the next generation."

This is a concept we should always have in the back of our minds. Always think about how you can help others. It doesn't even have to be anything big or take a lot of effort. Even holding doors for an elderly person takes minimal time and effort and will be highly appreciated by them.

God wants us to be a vessel of hope. He wants us to bless others, not tear them down or belittle them with our words or actions.

Do what you can to be a blessing to others. A simple word of encouragement. Provide a good reference to someone trying to get a job. Pay the coffee for the person in front of you. Smile back to someone when they say hello. It doesn't need to be anything big. You never know how far these blessings that you give to others will go.

Take the focus off yourself. Stop posting photos of yourself on social media constantly and seek out others to help, to give them a lift in their lives. Give credit to others. This shows good leadership, and others will respect you for the effort to recognize their efforts.

As martial arts instructors, we offer something different, something unique that is meant to be an avenue to improvement of mind, body, and spirit. If our focus is on ourselves, we are not providing a good example of the purpose of not only martial arts, but life in general.

ARTISTS

"I think there are two kinds of people in the world: creators and criticizers." The author of this quote, Mark Batterson, wrote this in his book *In a Pit with a Lion on a Snowy Day*.

I think I have a good idea of what's possibly going through your mind reading Batterson's quote. I'm just not the artistic type. I couldn't create a decent piece of art if my life depended on it!

However, I don't believe Batterson is talking about 'creators' from a purely artistic sense. He is referring to the type of person who makes things happen by taking the initiative. Someone who isn't sitting around and waiting for things to happen. And when they don't or if something good happens for someone else, then criticizing those people for their 'luck' or 'opportunity.' This applies to all things in life: sports, work, starting a business, and martial arts.

What is the purpose or what comes to mind when you consider a martial artist? Is a true artist someone who does the same thing repeatedly? Does a true artist reach a certain level and then sit back and feel like they have it all figured out? If you believe so, it's time to re-think your answer. An artist continually seeks to challenge themselves. They try to continually push the limits and seek new paths as they know this is the only way to growth. Artists need exposure to many different examples and ways to approach the arts to expand what the mind needs to grow and expand its limits.

Although my main art forum is Japanese Shodo, I soon realized that delving into other types of art such as abstract can bring new and different experiences into my Shodo work. Combining the two can enhance the overall visual experience and serve to help me grow as an artist.

Some may criticize this combination of abstract and traditional Shodo. Let them. Real growth only comes from trying to create something new, something interesting. Those who criticize are the ones who only wish they could instead be the creator.

To be an artist you must have the creative spirit. You need to *want* to do something new and try things that will challenge you. And you may fail miserably at first.

Artist Erik Wahl, a speed painter and public speaker, wanted to combine his artistic talents with a public speaking format to create something new and fresh to get across messages of the creative process for corporations.

Wahl was a keynote speaker at an ISACA conference I attended in 2018. His combination of speed painting to music and video images playing in tandem was fascinating. His performance inspired me to try abstract painting to which I've gained a fair degree of skill and confidence. When you see Wahl perform, it's surprising to learn that on his first attempt at his new style of public speaking was a massive failure.

He recounts that day in his book *The Spark and the Grind*, "I flailed like a fool and painted garbage. My ideas were disconnected and out of sync with the crowd. I was worried. But I was not deterred. What I lacked in talent, I made up for in passion. I was curious enough to keep trying and I was foolish enough not to quit."

This statement speaks volumes with how an artist thinks. Things may fall flat early on or even from time to time after a high degree of skill is obtained. But the idea is never to stop searching, experimenting, exploring, and working to push the envelope of your talents. An artist is never satisfied with where things currently stand nor with the status quo.

A true martial artist should be no different. When you look at leaders in martial arts, very often you will see some form of artistic background. Three gentlemen with whom I train and have formed their system of martial arts called Chi-Ryu Jiujitsu all have such a background. Isham Latimer is a painter and musician and studied art at SUNY University. John Costanzo is a graphic designer and is now venturing into photoshop. John McDonald is an actor and a screenplay writer.

All three men utilize their creative background and experiences within their martial arts, which paid dividends into their exploration and formulation of their system. They can utilize their artistic passion which Erik Wahl speaks about to venture onward and beyond the standard training methods to enhance their existing skills.

Artists look to bring their art mindset and practice into everyday life. Their approach to their craft and their way of thinking within their art practice isn't placed on a shelf when they put down their brush, or instrument, or pen.

This process should apply to martial arts as well. Miyamoto Musashi states in *The Book of Five Rings*, "The true science of martial arts means practicing them in such a way that they will be useful at any time, and to teach them in such a way that they will be useful in all things."

Whether you are engaged in your martial arts or not, your approach and mindset should be similar. As a martial arts instructor I try to relate the various concepts of movement to other sports to increase understanding within the student.

Conversely, if you have a background in other sports, such as golf, baseball, football, or tennis, then bringing the principles of those movements to your martial arts training can dramatically increase your ability to unlock the intricacies of movement in your martial arts training. This way of approaching your training is how artists think. Taking a slice out of the mindset of an artist can take your progress much farther than you may realize.

THANKFULNESS

Every experience, positive or negative, leads to learning and growth. And there are no accidents regarding all the experiences you encounter. Afterward, are you appreciative or thankful for the experience? Do you realize that the experience was meant to be beneficial to your overall development as a person?

When you think about it and put everything into perspective, problems and difficulties help to mold and strengthen you to take advantage of future issues and hurdles. Many times, we simply quit when faced with mounting problems, stress, and anxiety.

However, what if those things are in front of you to help you? Maintaining a position of thankfulness even in the bad and challenging times will help you keep everything in perspective.

In your martial arts training and experiences, be thankful for everything that comes across your path. In 1984 during my very first competition as a newly minted black belt, I faced in the second round of *kumite*, or sparring division, a highly seasoned black belt. His name was Carl Martin.

Master Martin is a great martial artist who would eventually be inducted into the International Isshinryu Hall of Fame in 2003. The last time I had seen him was when he was a visitor at my dojo when I had been training for only about six months.

I remembered he was extremely intimidating. His speed and power could be felt across the room and he was all business. Seeing him walk into the ring as my opponent several years later wasn't exactly the way I envisioned my black belt competitive days would begin. In short, I was taken to school that day.

Although frustrated and embarrassed, it didn't take me long to realize afterward that I'd just been in the ring with an amazing martial artist and fighter. I was thankful for the experience! How often do you get a chance to compete against one of the best?

In my first tournament right out of the gate I had gotten that opportunity and the experience and feedback was priceless. The problems and difficulties I encountered in the ring against Master Martin that day helped mold my competitive spirit.

Mark Batterson writes in his book *Double Blessing* that we tend to underappreciate God's attention to detail. He provides in his book one of the maxims he follows, "Whatever you don't turn into praise turns into pride." Always take time to be thankful.

Batterson adds, "One of the simplest ways to position ourselves for future blessings is by praising God for past blessings."

Take the time to reflect upon past experiences, both positive and negative, to provide perspective and to remind you how lucky you are to be where you are right now.

When I was in my late teens as a young black belt, I attended a seminar by the legendary fighter Joe Lewis. I heard other, more experienced martial artists discuss his skills and fighting record in the full-contact ring; however, I'd never seen him before the seminar. I wasn't sure exactly how good he really was.

The day of the seminar, to my surprise, he picked me to be his demonstration partner for the various techniques and concepts he wanted to teach that day. One of those techniques was using quick footwork to incorporate a straight leading jab to the face. He told me that he was going to tap my forehead with his fingertips and that I should try to block his front jab.

Try as I might, I simply could not react fast enough to block any of them. He made a comment to everyone regarding my complete strikeout, so to speak, to which everyone chuckled. It didn't bother me. I had a front row seat to what was being taught by a martial arts legend.

After doing some further research on Joe Lewis after the seminar, it began to dawn on me just how special of a martial artist he really was. I knew I was blessed to have had the opportunity to work with someone of his caliber, and I'm thankful those memories stick with me nearly 40 years later.

Being thankful helps to increase and maintain your energy levels. Norman Vincent Peale makes the point in *The Power of Positive Thinking*, "If the individual takes reasonable care of his body from the standpoint of proper diet, exercise, sleep, no physical abuse, the body will produce and maintain astonishing energy and sustain itself in good health. If he gives similar attention to a well-balanced emotional life, energy will be conserved."

One of the best ways to improve and keep a good emotional life is simply to be thankful in all things. Thankfulness will keep your spirits at a high level and energy will be there for you when you need it. Take the opposite approach and complain about everything, argue most of the time with others, or let little things frustrate you needlessly then your energy will be sapped very quickly.

Negativity will hurt your emotional well-being and suffocate any chance of sustaining any type of energy to do the things that you either need or want to do. Therefore, take the position of thankfulness as much as you can in your martial arts training and experiences – both good and bad. From this point of view, you will likely grow mentally, physically, and spiritually.

The problems and difficulties I encountered in the ring ... helped mold my competitive spirit.

PROCESS

Process is a concept that is different for everyone. The difference can be as varied as the differences between all of us. As it should be. We are all at different points along the path. Adapting your process to suit your style and needs keeps the focus on continuous improvement. Once you try to follow someone else's process, you lose what matters most to yourself.

The objective in your training, and in life, should be to continually search for efficiency and better ways of practicing your chosen field or endeavor. If you continually practice inefficiently or incorrectly, you will stagnate in your development.

The legendary golfer Ben Hogan is a true example of continuously looking for a better way of doing things. He relentlessly pursued how to improve his golf swing to the point of near fanaticism. In his book *The Modern Fundamentals of Golf*, he touches upon the purpose of improving your process and practicing with correct technique.

He writes, "…it really cuts me up to watch some golfer sweating over his shots on the practice tee, throwing away his energy to no constructive purpose, nine times out of 10 doing the same thing wrong he did years and years back when he first took up golf. This sort of golfer obviously loves the game, or he wouldn't be out there practicing it. I cannot watch him long. His frustration – all that fruitless expenditure of energy – really bothers me…the golfer who goes about this wisely will play good golf and should go on to enjoy his golf increasingly the rest of his life. The greatest pleasure is obtained by improving."

The entire gist behind this quote is on the 'process' of doing things efficiently and better to improve yourself. It doesn't matter the pursuit – your process, as defined by you, should be to take incremental steps to continually improve.

There are some general phases to consider regarding any process, though. When you are younger, the process tends to focus on yourself. As author Jason S.D. Perry points out in his book *An Old Man's Way*, "A young karate-ka must necessarily focus on technique and develop his or her own way. The focus is more on a personal acquisition of the *Jutsu* (art) of karate and less on the *Do* (way). Competition is often a part of the young man's way because it gives the karate-ka a sense of personal accomplishment and validation."

Perry goes on to explain that younger martial artists tend to visit other schools both within their organization and to outside schools to train and experience the atmosphere of the dojo away from their 'home' dojo. This is an essential part of the process in the development of your karate skills at the younger phase of your training. The same process can be said of many other forms or styles of martial arts.

Kendo, or the way of the sword, is an art where this process is critical. Hiroshi Ozawa provides very insightful dialogue on this topic in his book *Kendo, The Definitive Guide*. Ozawa explains, "If you always perform *keiko* (practice) at the same dojo with the same opponents, it is inevitable that your pitch of tension will eventually slacken and your keiko lose its freshness.

When this happens, you can bring about an increased sense of tension and revitalize your keiko by going to another dojo, or even to a completely different region. By going in the summer to somewhere with an even hotter climate, or in the winter to an even colder climate than your own, and by carrying out *shugyo* (student living with the teacher) in these places, you are exposed to a new kind of hardship.

Once you have overcome this, however, your confidence will increase enormously. By doing so again and again you will see an improvement in technical skills, as well as great spiritual benefits. Above all, it will make you richer and more rounded as a person."

This same idea to training applies to nearly every type of endeavor you can think of. It is quite difficult to improve your golf game by playing the same course over and over. Insert your sport of choice into the prior sentence – it still applies. Likewise, it is challenging to improve as a martial artist by training in the same school as well as competing at the same tournament all the time. Your process should include diversity in what you are exposed to in order to keep your skills sharp.

As you get older the process tends to flip over into helping others. As Perry goes on to write of his father's development, "With Perry Sensei's maturation as a karate-ka, his karate has become less about himself and more about developing others...His focus has shifted from developing his own combative skills to a pursuit of preserving the art of karate..."

In effect, the process changes by recognizing the changes in yourself. It is impossible to maintain the same exact process throughout your entire life since your mind and body change considerably over time. Even though you cannot perform your karate the same from a physical perspective, you can preserve your martial art by helping others and teaching your art to the next generation of students. And this passing on of knowledge doesn't necessarily always stem from being able to perform the same way as you did as a young person.

The joy in your chosen field – whether it's a sport, hobby, or your profession - is in the process, not in the destination. The reason: once you reach your destination, what is left?

IMMERSION

There is no exact science or textbook on immersing yourself into your specific field of interest. I was asked by a friend of mine in 2007 if I would like to have a gallery show for my Shodo artwork. He had an acquaintance who owned a gallery. My immediate reaction was, "That's great but I'm not quite ready for anything like that. I need more time to continue improving my work."

The truth behind those words were that I had no clue how to go about preparing for and presenting my Shodo art in a gallery setting and making it look professional. Even though in the back of my mind that was something I always wanted to try, I was reluctant because I had never done it before, and I was nervous it wouldn't come out looking like my artwork even belonged there.

I figured I needed to do a bunch of research on just the steps regarding the setup process and the administration side of things alone. I imagined there had to be a book or resource on such things…and maybe there are. But most often there are lessons that can only be learned outside of a classroom or a textbook.

You must learn some lessons the hard way by just getting in the arena and immersing yourself into the action. Jump in with both feet and get wet without thinking too much about it to begin with. Ever notice how they train infants to swim? They simply put them in the water and off they go. There's no worry or anxiety over the process beforehand.

Immerse yourself and learn as you go. Two years after that initial request for a gallery show, I was thinking about it again during a practice session with my Shodo. I just thought it's now or never. I called my friend back regarding the potential for a showing, and after checking, he noted the gallery was still interested. I did the gallery show, and I made a ton of mistakes. I believe I had too many pieces stuffed into a small area. My informational handout on the artwork was a bit long.

Being on the second floor, I had an area of the gallery that had a low amount of foot traffic. The list of mistakes went on and on. I took mental notes as well as jotting things down on paper afterwards. I learned a lot of valuable lessons. My next show was the following year at the same gallery. I was much more relaxed about everything. I was confident in myself because I knew I would not make the same mistakes again.

I requested a better area of the gallery to display my work. I made slight adjustments in the setup and, sure enough, this show was received very well. There were positive news articles posted, and I ended up selling quite a few pieces over the weekend. Clearly, the process of immersing myself into an art gallery show paid dividends. If you jump into something knowing full well there will be mistakes made, removing the pressure of expecting everything to go perfectly, then you will benefit immensely.

You must throw yourself into whatever it is you are hesitant to try. You cannot improve by watching entirely from the sidelines. Granted, observation is a key component to improvement in anything. But without getting into the action, you are missing crucial feedback with all the human senses.

Regardless of what it is you have interest in, think about how to immerse yourself more fully into the subject. If you take up photography, don't simply go out and start taking pictures. Research into the various products on the market. Join a photography club or chat group and connect with others with varying degrees of skill and experiences that can help you along the way.

Consider a trip to a place that has always interested you based on what you've seen. If you like the work of Ansel Adams, then travel to the same locations he used and immerse yourself there. Compare your work to his and see what's different. See what looks close in style and presentation. Consider how you can adjust your process the next time to capture something a bit different than what Adams did.

If you take up a new sport such as running or a new activity such as painting, the same thought processes apply.

Of course, the process of immersion applies to martial arts training as well. There's an expression that you need to rub elbows with those more experienced than yourself. Only then will you pick up bits and pieces of information that you can absorb into your own training and your own advancement of skill.

Watch higher ranked practitioners train and see if you can pick up little details that sets them apart. Listen to casual conversations and ask specific questions. Attend open tournaments and watch competitors from other disciplines and organizations. What are some of the things they are doing to be successful?

Introduce yourself to new people and discuss their training and their tournament preparation. You may uncover some interesting tips that you can apply to your own training program. Use the technology at your fingertips to capture movements that you can review repeatedly. In the latest system which I'm training, I very often record my instructors on my cell phone. I can then replay the techniques and forms at home whenever I want, and what I learned in person is not lost.

Immerse yourself fully into your chosen martial art, activity, or sport. The more you search and consider various ways to enhance your experiences, the more rewarding it will be over the long haul. Those who reach a certain level and believe they've arrived are selling themselves short of what could be achieved. Immersion means there are no end goals, but rather the activity defines who you are.

ACCOUNTABILITY

I've always enjoyed Japanese calligraphy artwork. So, I finally worked up the nerve and asked my Kendo sensei to teach me *Shodo*, or calligraphy. It took several attempts but he reluctantly agreed. He reminded me the difficulty of such an art form and the practice that Shodo demanded. But my mind was set. I'd thought about taking up Shodo ever since I'd seen it displayed in his apartment along with his brushes and various books on this art on his living room table.

At the first lesson on a Saturday morning at 7:00 am before the Kendo students showed up, he brushed the character for *mizu* (水), or water. There are only four brushstrokes to this kanji but for a beginner, believe me when I tell you this is plenty to handle. I kept looking at his sample and tried my best to duplicate it. Of course, I came nowhere near to making my completed character look like my instructor's work.

After 30 minutes of practice, sensei told me to put everything away and get ready for Kendo class. He told me to practice for the next week and to prepare the *mizu* kanji for his review at the next class. I thought to myself that if I really want to learn Shodo, then I'll have to be accountable for practicing on my own. I may not have my instructor with me each time I practice, but I will do the best I can knowing that mistakes are part of the learning process.

The first couple of months of my Shodo experience was beyond frustrating. When I practiced at home my work looked almost like primitive stick figures. No matter how much I concentrated and tried to make my brushstrokes appear the same as my sensei's sample from the prior lesson, it always looked like a complete failure. It was a major struggle to get the proper look of the character just right.

The thought of bailing out on this goal and quitting would creep up on me. But each time, I kept telling myself that my sensei is giving of his time and effort to teach me. I have to be accountable to both myself and my teacher. I just had to keep practicing and putting in the repetitions. Just like learning anything new, the more times you do something the better and more comfortable you'll be. I told myself why should Shodo be any different?

Eventually, I would begin to acquire the proper technique to make my calligraphy get closer and closer to the actual sample brushed by my sensei. Being accountable and putting in the repetitions helped me to develop the proper handling of the brush, a more relaxed mind and breathing, the right amount of pressure from brush to paper, and the ability to slow down when the character called for a change in direction.

Accountability occurs when you get your heart right and understand that without being accountable to yourself and others, then progress is nearly impossible. You can handle whatever you set your mind to. But whatever it is you want to do—in any aspect of life—someone else is likely involved. You need to understand that your actions have consequences. If you don't realize you're accountable to someone else, then your pursuits will likely not mean anything.

In the martial arts, the relationship between the sensei and the student is a two-way street. As the student, you are accountable to your teacher in that you need to continually practice and work to improve your techniques and your overall understanding of the art. If you're not practicing regularly or you have excuse after excuse as to why you're not in class, then you're not being accountable to your instructor.

As the instructor, you are accountable to your students. You need to continually work on your lesson plans to keep the material fresh and interesting. You need to always be at class and ready to impart the various aspects of the art whether you feel like it or not. You are accountable to your students as they are relying on your guidance and look to you to set the example of hard work and consistency. If you're not accountable, then the students will quickly notice and find another place to train.

A good teacher will hold their students accountable. They will give the student specific things to work on between classes. They should set forth sound principles and rules to follow in daily life to maintain their training status. At times, it may seem like a lot of work. But that's what accountability does. It makes you work to achieve the goals you put upon yourself.

———————◆———————

You need to understand
that your actions have consequences.
If you don't realize you're accountable to someone else, then your pursuits will likely
not mean anything.

YOUR MIND IN TRAINING

You need to be aware of just how much your mind plays an important role in your training. Keeping your thoughts positive tends to lead toward the results that you seek. You need to think big; however, more importantly, you must continually think upon and reflect on the process. You need to think about specific steps to take to get to where you want to go.

And you should incorporate into this process the time to visualize yourself going through those steps repeatedly to solidify the positive mindset needed to achieve your goals. Author Gary Keller makes this case in his book *The One Thing*, "In three separate studies, psychologists observed 262 students to see the impact of visualization on outcomes. The students were asked to visualize the outcome (like getting an "A" on an exam) and others were asked to visualize the process needed to achieve a desired outcome (like all of the study sessions needed to earn that "A" on the exam). In the end, students who visualized the process performed better across the board – they studied earlier and more frequently and earned higher grades than those who simply visualized the outcome."

When it comes to my writing, I utilize the 'stepped' approach as this has proven time and again to be successful to reach the end goal: publishing a book. I can set all the goals and timelines I want such as *I want this project to be published by the end of the year.* But unless I develop concrete, definitive steps to reach that goal I will procrastinate and find other things to occupy my day.

I know from experience that I need to consciously set aside a specific time every day to work on the writing project without fail. Regardless of the productivity on any given day, following the steps precisely is the main objective to reach the final goal. This way of training your mind applies to anything you wish to accomplish in life.

With respect to your martial arts, while driving to the dojo think about having a great class and what it is you need to work on to improve a specific technique or sequence in a form you are learning. Envision yourself performing those movements better and better. Until you can see yourself performing your techniques at a high level, it will become difficult to make that become a reality. You must repeat that positive image over and over again in your mind, both in slow motion and in normal speed.

This is where video can be a valuable resource in your training. If you're struggling with a particular kata, or form, then watch a highly skilled martial artist on video. There's no need to wait until you work with your instructor again. I have students learning *Arnis*, the Philippine art of stick fighting. I always encourage them to look up others on YouTube and repeatedly watch their videos. Watching their movements and then visualizing yourself doing those techniques and combinations will make a difference.

Mixing up your training process can also train and push your mind into higher levels. Get creative in your approach to practicing your art. Develop unusual drills to challenge yourself as much as possible. Try other forms of physical activity to supplement what you are doing in the dojo. Yoga, weight training, running, hiking and Pilates are just a few examples.

My older daughter recently started Pure Barre and eventually became a certified instructor. Pure Barre is a new type of fitness program which is a total body workout focused on low impact but high intensity movements that improves strength and flexibility. Hearing her explain a specific workout and how your need to hold various postures, similar to yoga, I immediately looked to see how breathing plays a role in Pure Barre and how that ties into a martial arts system that I practice called Chi-Ryu Jiujitsu.

One of the main principles of Chi-Ryu Jiujitsu is proper breathing to develop mind, body, and spirit. There are several exercises to develop this aspect of the art that are meant to be practiced daily. Exploring the importance of breathing from another form of exercise and how it is applied was a logical step in my mind. It is this type of thinking and connection of various disciplines that can add to your overall development. Your mind must be open to explore these connections.

Another process to consider for improving your mind in your ongoing training, regardless of the martial art you are studying or any other form of activity, is to empty the mind. By this I mean emptying your mind of all negative thoughts. This leads to more peace of mind. When your mind is at peace, you can handle what is in front of you or what you are trying to improve upon.

Norman Vincent Peale explains in his book *The Power of Positive Thinking*, "A primary method for gaining a mind full of peace is to practice emptying the mind. Definitely practice emptying your mind of fears, hates, insecurities, regrets, and guild feelings."

We've all had a few of those examples. When you take personal inventory, you'll notice negativity from time to time in your martial arts training, your relationships, your work, and in your personal pursuits. Consciously setting aside time to empty your mind of these worries and problems will help considerably.

And this process doesn't necessarily have to be on the level of meditation. All it takes is several minutes of personal time and quiet if that's all you can provide. Control your breathing, make it deliberate and slow and on each exhale, visualize in your mind the negativity leaving your mind. As with anything, this daily practice will become easier over time.

In tandem with the process of emptying the mind, develop the habit of picturing in your mind success. Peale explains, "The basic factor in psychology is the realizable wish. The man who assumes success tends already to have success. People who assume failure tend to have failure. When either failure or success is picturized, it strongly tends to actualize in terms equivalent to the mental image pictured."

Of course, this is not an automatic or foolproof process. You must have complete confidence and trust that your positive image will come true. As some say, you need to be "all in." And you need to portray, or more importantly, display that positive picture in your mind every day. Peale includes in his book a quote from the famous psychologist William James, "Our belief at the beginning of a doubtful undertaking is the one thing that ensures the successful outcome of your venture."

I made the decision to run a marathon in 2015. I knew with complete confidence that if I followed my training plan down to the last detail, I would have no problem finishing the run. The dreaded 'did not finish', or DNF, that all runners fear never entered my mind. When you empty your mind of negative thoughts, continually post successful images in your mind, and you're all in, then positive results are just a matter of time.

What is it that ultimately leads your mind in a specific direction or gets you to pursue a goal or dream? Faith. Above all, you must have faith in yourself and see yourself succeeding to take action and move forward. Keller points out in *The One Thing* that faith leads to action, which in turn helps us avoid regrets. Having faith in yourself keeps your mind strong and helps you not to regret mistakes or errors, but to learn from them. When you can do this, then you know your mind is in the right place.

COMPETITION

I recently came upon a comment on social media: "True karate can never be a sport." However, competition provides a bar of measurement to which you can see where you stand in your progress. Many other endeavors are the same. You need competition to test yourself and put yourself in uncomfortable situations to test your mettle, to see for yourself what is needed on your part to overcome stress, anxiety, doubt, and fear.

Both of my daughters have been dancing since they were very little. And the younger is now in college pursuing a Bachelor of Fine Arts in dance. She is pursuing dance as a career and studying various styles of the art form. But I've heard many say that dance is not a sport. Yet, competitions are widespread with dancing. Can you compete in dance and develop your skills in the traditional aspects of dance at the same time? Of course. Competition and traditional training do not have to be mutually exclusive. And the same is true for traditional martial arts.

Those who are staunchly against any type of competition when it comes to their martial arts training have most likely been fed negativity towards such endeavors time and time again; thus, they believe such statements. When you look around and take notice of which martial artists continue their advancement in the various budo, one common denominator is that they all were frequent competitors on the open tournament circuit.

Think not of only famous martial artists, but of those around you who contribute to the arts whether it's publishing articles or books, studying other systems to incorporate into their own training, or those who are developing new training ideas and systems of martial arts. Chances are very high that they competed heavily at one point or another in their martial arts journey. This is not by mistake.

If you compete seriously, you are forced to figure out how to overcome your fellow competitors. How do I get my technique off a split second before the other guy in sparring? How do I defend the opponent who always seems to win every tournament with kicks that are lightning fast? How can I get the judges to notice my kata performance, especially when I seem to go first all the time?

Competition gets you to reflect on these challenges and figure out a way to perform better each time you compete. Over time, you can see how this leads to higher levels of exploration within the traditional aspects of the martial arts. The need to increase your skills, understanding, and potential is directly proportional to your competitive days as a traditional martial artist.

For purposes of this book, we will discuss competition and preparation for kata competition. Kata competition requires the form to have functionality while at the same time ensuring the movements and techniques look appealing. Pay attention to every detail to make sure you have complete understanding of the movements and a strong, captivating spirit not only with every movement but with each pause in the action.

One idea to improve kata performance, while at the same time improving your overall martial arts skills, is to pick a different kata or form every year to compete exclusively with. For the entire tournament year, you will work on that one specific kata and compete every time with that specific form. This approach will create a mindset and a commitment to excel with that form. Your singular efforts in training to improve your chosen kata will develop a high degree of skill.

Regardless of your success with another kata or form from the previous year, you must stick to your decision and train relentlessly with your current kata. This will help you become a well-rounded martial artist because every year you are focusing on a new kata that contains new techniques and new possibilities in your performance. In essence, this approach forces new growth in your technical skills and mental capacity. You realize there is no turning back, and you commit to the new kata through thick and thin.

With kata, you are telling a story through your performance of the movements and techniques. Therefore, you need to think about and figure out how to get the judges to see and believe your story. You need to sell the judges on your performance and your ability to stand out.

Often, competitions have many competitors and many of them are performing the same kata or form as you are. You must find out how to become different than everyone else in the crowd. You need to bring a level of confidence that all other competitors are not able to demonstrate.

To assist in this development, break down the kata into smaller, more manageable sequences that you can work on over and over. Find out through trial and error what works and what doesn't work. Very often, slow is smooth and smooth is fast. You cannot be tight and expect your performance to come across as visually impressive.

Look at a professional baseball player who has a good swing and is successful. They are not tense in the batter's box, and they don't rely upon their muscular strength. Rather, they are relaxed, and their swing is smooth and controlled. The same can be said for professional golfers.

For your kata performance with respect to the execution of the actual techniques, there should be a natural rhythm and flow. The kata should not be performed robotically with the same amount of time between pauses, turns, and combinations. There needs to be explosive moves coupled with pauses at various times to break up the rhythm.

If you think in terms of music, the performance needs to be more staccato, or up and down, versus a monotone rhythm. The rhythm needs to change to tell a compelling story of the fight and the demonstration of your strong points. All these concepts can be worked on when you break down the kata into segments or sequences of moves. It will take much practice and introspection to develop this varying rhythm.

The competition doesn't begin when you are called up to perform your kata or form. It begins when you enter the ring. You need to appear ready and project the spirit that you are completely ready and confident in your abilities. The argument could also be made that impressions begin the moment you take the floor with your karate gi, or uniform.

As you are warming up prior to the competition, you never know whether the black belts in proximity will be officials in your ring. If you practice and warm up with a total command of your body, mind, and spirit, it can serve several benefits. First, it can show your fellow competitors that they are in for a long day. If they are nowhere near your level of preparation, it will show when they see you warm up. Second, if there are black belts nearby witnessing your warm-up that is performed at a high level, they will remember that when it comes time to score your performance.

Cross training is another potential area that can improve your competition performance and potential results. There are a multitude of endeavors that can help you such as running or walking, yoga, weightlifting and even learning or studying formal dance. Anything that can improve your overall training program is something to consider in your quest to put together the best competition performance you can.

Tips and tricks are nice, but you need to put in the work to be competitive, remain competitive, and eventually overcome your rivals in competition. It's a long and difficult road. But if you make the sacrifices and work towards your goals, it will be the catalyst that allows you to become the martial artist that you can become.

You need to think about specific steps to take to get to where you want to go.

INJURIES

Most of us have faced an injury of some sort throughout our training process, whether that was for martial arts or another sport. Injuries can derail your training plans and goals in a heartbeat. Even worse, they can sometimes be so depressing that they overcome you mentally leading to eventually quitting the activity altogether.

I've had my share of them. Arthroscopic surgery on my right knee. Anterior cruciate ligament reconstruction on my left knee. Frozen left shoulder surgery. All these injuries and subsequent surgeries leading to 12-14 weeks of physical therapy. How do you deal with the frustration of injuries? How do you continue training intelligently to overcome the setbacks that injuries throw on you?

There are several well-known sayings regarding injury and pain: "No pain, no gain." "Pain is weakness leaving the body." Hey, whatever keeps you going. But most of us are not engaged in our respective activity to pay the bills. Even if we were a professional athlete, have you noticed how often players at that level are on the 'injured list'?

In this modern sporting age, players are an investment, and the investment must be protected. Therefore, any sign of discomfort and they're not in the lineup. We are not professionally paid athletes; however, we need to invest in ourselves as there is nothing more frustrating than not taking part in the action.

When an injury does show up unexpectedly, it's the mind that really comes into play to help you pull through and eventually get back in the game. From this perspective a variety of attributes need to surface. You need to be patient as time is the only thing that matters at this point. Time is what is needed to heal yet the clock ticks slower and slower in your mind.

Patience needs to be improved as there is no other choice in most instances. Intelligence needs to surface during this time. You should reflect upon what could have possibly led up to the injury in the first place. Sitting around waiting until you're healed, returning to activity in the same manner, and re-injuring yourself along the way is simply not a smart way to go. Learning from your situation is a far better approach to avoid future injury and, even better, you could be a resource to others if they ever get injured in a manner similar to your experiences.

During your recovery phase is a time to reassess your goals and your training timeline. Was your training schedule too aggressive? Did you overlook critical recovery aspects of your training plan? Look at your actions prior to the injury from all angles. Discuss it with others and compare notes to see where possibly your training was a bit off-track and make corrections. Use your mind in a variety of ways to take advantage of the learning opportunities during your injury recovery.

Don't waste the time being frustrated or depressed. The injury most likely happened for a reason. Find out why.

Most importantly, injury will tap into an area of your life that is critical – your spirit. Will you break, or will you overcome? You quickly realize that often, it is not just you that will come back from the injury. Your need to ensure your faith is strong as your life and the ability to bounce back is in God's hands. Suffering from an injury, when having the proper perspective, can do wonders to strengthen you spiritually.

In his book *Suffering*, author Paul David Tripp provides these thoughts, "Physical suffering exposes the delusion of personal autonomy and self-sufficiency. If you and I had the kind of control that we fall into thinking we have, none of us would ever go through anything difficult. None of us would choose to be sick. None of us would choose to experience physical pain. None of us likes the prospect of being physically weak and disabled. None of us likes our lives being put on hold. Physical suffering does force you to face the reality that your life is in the hands of another. It reminds you that you are small and dependent, that whatever little bits of power and control you have can be taken away in an instant. Independence is a delusion that is quickly exposed by suffering."

So, it's important how we react to injuries and the subsequent suffering that goes along with it. As Tripp further explains, "Your responses to the situations in your life, whether physical, relational, or circumstantial, are always more determined by what is inside you (your heart) than by the things you are facing."

After an initial period of disappointment due to missing a goal or a big event and coming to terms with the setback stemming from an injury, it's important to get your heart right and tap into your faith. How you react will strongly determine, if not fully determine, how you'll overcome the injury and quite possibly come back better than ever.

Above all, the injury likely took place to teach you something about yourself. Your reaction and how you come to terms with it will be instructional to those around you. You may come back from it fully recovered or you'll simply use the injury as an excuse to put in the hard work necessary to overcome it. Or most likely, somewhere between the two. One thing is certain. The injury will surely change you. How you deal with it will help shape the quality of the rest of your life.

Do what you can to be a blessing to others.

A simple word of encouragement.

Pay for the coffee for the person
in front or behind you.

Smile back to someone when they say hello.

It doesn't need to be anything big.

You never know how far these blessings that
you give to others will go

KATA

The translation of *kata* (kah tah) in martial arts is - form. Wikipedia explains kata as "a detailed choreographed pattern of martial arts movements made to be practiced alone." There are complete books on the subject of kata from the perspective of the complete kata taught within a specific system, from a historical perspective, as well as from a research and study frame of reference. Kata is arguably the basis and foundation for all martial arts. If the sword is the soul of the samurai, then kata might very well be the soul of the karate-ka.

Although most agree regarding the importance of kata in learning martial arts, the very topic can be a point of fierce disagreement and debate as well. Many people adhere to the interpretations, or *bunkai*, of the movements within kata as they were taught by their sensei from when they first learned a particular kata. This is perfectly acceptable and often the purpose behind maintaining the moves without change is to simply honor the sensei for what they imparted on the student. Of course, the interpretations can vary widely from school to school and even within the same system, which brings a form of disagreement into the mix. Add to that, sometimes high-ranking students from the same instructor may change some bunkai to suit their own needs as time goes on. Thus, the debates get even further tangled.

I believe we, as martial artists, need to step back from time-to-time and reflect on kata and what some of the main purposes are for learning them. Even here, many people have a hard time agreeing upon the purpose of kata. There could be several based upon who you discuss the topic with.

Kata can represent the various movements that the founder of the system thought were most beneficial to help students learn their particular martial art. Some may call those movements combative skills while others would argue the movements are meant to tell a story, so to speak, of the background behind the kata such as terrain and so forth.

Others will explain that kata are more abstract in nature and are simply combinations of kicks, punches, and blocks. It's how you perform those movements that matter. One time may be full force and power, and another time may be more along the lines of flowing from Tai Chi. Still other comments may be along the lines that kata are simply another method of practice to assist with overall development. As previously stated, it depends on who you talk to and what your instructor focuses on in the teaching of a particular martial art.

With all of this in mind, I think many can agree that as a student holding rank below black belt, you should learn what your instructor is teaching. Upon earning the black belt, which is considered more of a beginning than a destination in the martial arts, you should realized that there is so much more to the martial arts.

At this point in your training, all the thoughts on kata mentioned above come into play. If you happen to run your own school, there is a fine line to walk – teaching what your sensei intends to be taught within the boundaries of your system while at the same time exploring alternatives and researching on your own to find *your* truth.

I hold the belief that *not every move, in every kata, is meant for everyone.* The founder of my main system of karate, Isshinryu, was approximately five feet tall. I'm six feet two inches. Everyone is different in size and abilities. Learning kata a specific way prior to black belt makes sense, mainly from the perspective of learning the art in its pure form.

However, black belt level marks the beginning of exploration and how to make the techniques effective for yourself. For me to make certain techniques work that a man who stood five feet tall is a big ask, especially as time goes on and the body changes naturally regarding what it can perform.

Additionally, I feel as though the kata resemble a template for what the founder of a particular system wanted his students to know. At a certain point of proficiency, students should be expected to take that template and work with it further. Use the kata and explore different methods of movement, different applications of the same movements, and push the limits further and further.

I truly believe kata are a part of the process to advance ourselves as martial artists. Without further exploration and seeking better methods of performance and more tactically sound applications based on your current physical abilities, I feel we are doing a disservice to our martial arts forefathers.

They improved upon their training methods and developed new systems and applications. Should we not do the same? Should we perform our kata the same way we did 10 years ago? Should we keep the interpretations frozen in time and never seek new ways of applying techniques? Should we never discover better ways of making something effective within our forms?

The famous Shotokan karate master Shigeru Egami said, "Despite a lack of complete understanding, one should not assume that the movements have no meaning or function. I advise performing the movements, thinking about them, and interpreting them in your own way, concentrating heart and soul."

Progression as a martial artist *requires* exploration and adapting techniques to work for you. We are all different. But how do we blend honoring our instructors by keeping their teachings going while at the same time opening our minds and training methods to a more progressive approach? As a martial artist, pondering these questions should capture a good bit of your attention.

Then there are the lessons beyond merely the physical aspects of kata such as strong techniques and what it is you are doing within the movements. There is the mental side of kata, which requires sharpening of your instincts during performance to mirror, as closely as possible, an actual fighting or self-defense encounter.

After a kata is learned, there should be no teaching of proper posture or allowance of training aids for the student to transition from inability to perform a movement properly. Posture is learned while performing basics repetitively until it is a natural thing.

Kata is for performing an actual fight. The famous karate master and pioneer Chosin Chibana stated, "There is no posture in karate kata. Except for the beginning and the end of the kata. Everything else is transition and application."

The practitioner must begin to use creativity to express the encounter not only with motion but also with proper breathing, proper mental projection of your intentions, and proper usage of pauses and looks just prior to engaging the next opponent. You should explore the rhythm and tempo of your motions to determine the best motion for yourself. The 'fight' must be created, and it must not only be convincing in the moment, it should evolve over time with the evolution of the martial artists themselves.

Never changing or adapting the movements and techniques in kata over time is fine. People feel they need to preserve the history of the founders of the kata. However, kata were created by people. Creators and artists develop their craft to get those who observe their art to think and touch their spirit in some way. Take their creation when the time is right and move it forward.

In the case of kata, adapt the techniques to work for you. The meaning behind every technique cannot be the same for everyone. We are all different, and we all change over time. If I try to perform the same meaning as someone else, then I'm not creating or exploring, I'm simply imitating.

MOVEMENT

Movement is everywhere. Even when you think there's no movement physically such as when your sleeping, there is still movement within your respiratory and circulatory systems. Stand at an overlook area along a highway or pause and observe the valley below during a hike along the ridge of a mountain. Motion will come into view soon enough from people on the ground, the wind rustling the leaves around you, and from the birds and squirrels in proximity. Movement cannot be escaped. Without it, there is no possibility of experiencing life.

Long distance runners and ultrarunners have a mantra: keep moving forward. When movement is graceful and effortless, such as within a dance or a martial arts form, it is captivating and inspirational. Movement can also be captured on paper. Whether the artist is a photographer or a painter, expressing movement in art can enrich the contemplative spirit of the observer. This could be why many in the United States are intrigued by Shodo, or Japanese calligraphy. A good example of Shodo can clearly demonstrate movement of the brush on paper.

In terms of the martial arts, movement most closely defines the concept of all skills and techniques as being open and flowing, where there is continuous flow of energy and motion. Several martial arts hinge upon the use of continuous motion including Tai Chi, Aikido, and the Filipino martial arts systems. All these arts are captivating to watch when performed at very high levels.

Regardless of the style, however, every skill or technique has one fundamental element at the genesis and that is *movement,* or more specifically, *unbroken motion.* The most efficient and effective manner of movement should be as natural as possible. This is accomplished by the level of coordination between mind, body, and breath, as the movements are performed.

There is a deceptive level of force in movement when these three elements are present and in harmony. This might be perceived as being something automatic. However, it is perhaps this aspect of coordination that is most difficult to learn and harness because to accomplish it one must move slowly, without ego, without intent, without stopping and starting, or with thoughts of winning and losing.

There is a saying: *Slow is smooth, smooth is fast, fast is deadly.* This concept applies in almost every area of life. When things get out of control...slow down.

The author Norman Vincent Peale tells the following story in his book *The Power of Positive Thinking,* "A former member of a championship university crew [rowing] told me that their shrewd crew coach often reminded them: "To win this or any race, row slowly." He pointed out that rapid rowing tends to break the stroke and when the stroke is broken it is with the greatest difficulty that crew recovers the rhythm necessary to win.

Meanwhile other crews pass the disorganized group. It is indeed wise advice – "To go fast, row slowly."

For sound movement in martial arts training, the intention is to eliminate the body and mind of tension during your movements. This allows for improved chi, or qi (energy), circulation essential to achieving a higher level of oxygen throughout the circulatory system. It is also a method for achieving better overall health. However, achieving this level of moving with energy takes considerable time and dedicated practice.

There must be continual effort to improve your muscles and flexibility in the first place, so when you understand the required physical exertion needed in combination with proper breathing, you can then conserve your energy properly while you move. Explore various methods of physical training including weightlifting, Pilates, isometrics, yoga, and various other cross training activities. Muscles need to be used to function properly to allow for sound movement. If you do not train them, it will be next to impossible to understand how to use them in the most efficient manner needed for longevity.

In tandem with muscular improvement and training, you need to explore how to breathe properly so when these two elements are combined properly the results are beneficial to your overall health.

In 2007, I started training with Master Isham Latimer in the martial art of Chi-Ryu Jiujitsu. This art uses as part of its foundation breathing exercises from Tai Chi. I thought the Tai Chi movements would blend quite

113

well with my background in Isshinryu, Modern Arnis, and Kendo. I soon found out how deceptively complex these breathing exercises really were. They were extremely uncomfortable at first. I was constantly being told, "Relax. Don't tense your fingers. Let them relax and allow the energy to flow. Keep the knees slightly bent."

All of this made sense and sounded easy enough, but at the end of 15 minutes of breathing exercises, my legs shook, and my feet hurt. I was used to moving around so standing still, relaxing, breathing and moving slow and deliberate was something that took time to adapt to.

Another benefit to focused attention on motion and proper breathing is internal strength – not from muscles, but rather from tendons and bones. Essentially, the structure of the body, which is unseen, is strengthened with slower, deliberate movement coupled with conscious and controlled breathing exercises.

The breathing exercises of Chi-Ryu Jiujitsu lends to the understanding of the concept that **when one thing moves, everything moves**. The coordination of mind, breath, tendons, and fascia allows the practitioner to move effortlessly with optimum effect in techniques delivered.

This is somewhat like those who participate in parkour. This newer activity requires free motion that can only be accomplished with a relaxed mind and breathing coupled with reliance upon the elasticity built into the body's tendons and fascia. If muscles are overly tense, leading to fatigue, the parkour enthusiast will suffer, and his motion will be short-lived. They must rely on the body's natural movement and elasticity to bounce from skill to skill.

The same holds true for the martial arts as well as most any other sport. If a professional baseball player is not relaxed and elastic in his movement when swinging the bat, it becomes quite difficult to perform the intended action against a ball traveling at 90+ miles per hour from 60 feet, six inches away. The same is true in golf. For those of us who are weekend hackers, we cannot make the ball go where we want to every time because we haven't developed the proper muscular control coupled with elasticity in our swing.

Breath control is your starting point for maintaining mental toughness as well as controlling the nervous system that is so essential in controlling movement and reaction. Exercise and movement are controlled and affected by the nervous system. A sound nervous system allows the muscles to stretch and contract in concert with your breathing. All of this is influenced by the mind; however, without proper breathing, the mind can override your nervous system and cause inappropriate movement or reactions. When you are calm, the body can remain relaxed. When you are relaxed you can then move both efficiently and effectively.

BREATHING

Breathing is a key ingredient to our survival, as we all know. We don't give breathing a second thought unless we're in an emergency situation or sickness is hampering our normal breathing in some way. However, breathing properly and why we should be doing it in the correct manner warrants more of our attention and awareness. This applies to everyone, but especially to those who rely on good breathing habits whether it's a sport or, most critically, in martial arts.

Martial arts consist of both external techniques such as physical motion and development along with internal concepts such as breathing, chi energy, and spiritual development. But it seems that quite a few martial arts focus on the external piece of the puzzle. Many styles include a form within their curriculum that contains dynamic muscular tension and breathing combined. But often these forms are creating a forced breathing pattern that can be counterintuitive as is explained later in the chapter.

Why are modern systems of martial arts dropping from their teachings the importance, understanding, and practice of proper breathing? It seems the internal aspects of training are given trivial amounts of time and consideration by current martial artists.

Dr. Yang, Jwing-Ming is a well-known Chinese martial artist, and he makes this point in his book *Qigong*, "When the Oriental martial arts were imported to the Western world, because of traditional secrecy, the modern life-style, and the different cultural background, there was a separation between the training of the external techniques and the internal cultivation. This has made the arts and the training incomplete."

Breathing properly in tandem with controlled movement is something that takes many years to learn, fully understand, and apply properly. Our society simply doesn't afford that kind of time. We need to *make* the time to practice this aspect of martial arts. Where you put your time correlates to what you find important. And many martial artists mistakenly overlook the importance of proper breathing.

It is unfortunate that modern martial artists are not giving proper breathing exercises more attention as the benefits are numerous. There must be a committed effort to continually think about and focus on your breathing to improve.

I train with the three developers of the Chi-Ryu Jiujitsu system. All three men are 70+ years in age, yet they have the physical attributes of men 25-30 years younger. They have incorporated breathing exercises like Tai Chi in their training for over 25 years. They also have within the training requirements a form from the internal system of Hsing-I Liuhe Bafa Chuan, a Chinese system that predates Tai Chi. If you are not breathing correctly, then completion of the Liuhe Bafa form is quite difficult to say the least.

Breath control is your starting point for maintaining mental toughness as well as controlling the nervous system that is so essential in controlling movement and reaction. The famous Shotokan karate master Hirokazu Kanazawa makes the point strongly regarding breath control in his book *Karate, My Life* where he states, "Ninety percent of people do not know how to breathe correctly. If your breathing is wrong, your body will be wrong, and your mind will be wrong."

As Mark Devine of SealFit points out on YouTube, "Proper breathing is where to begin in order to gain control over a situation." This may include fear, stress, anxiety, or worry. Devine also points out, "Every breath pattern has a corresponding emotional pattern to it. Fear leads to shortness of breath or panting, an erratic pattern."

When your mind takes over your thoughts leading to such things as fear, your breathing will suffer making it difficult to control what is at hand. You must control your breath which is the one thing you can rely on. Devine explains, "If you're not aware of your breath, then you're out of control. First action is to come back to the breath, and check in with it, develop an intimate awareness of it (slow it down)."

Everything begins with proper breathing and control over your breathing patterns. And the benefits go beyond self-defense techniques. There is considerable science behind breathing to support the benefits of proper breathing and the adverse effects of improper breathing. In a May 21, 2020 article in the *Wall Street Journal*, author James Nestor writes in the 'The Healing Power of Proper Breathing', "Breathing properly can allow us to live longer and healthier lives. Breathing poorly, by contrast, can exacerbate and sometimes cause a laundry list of chronic diseases: asthma, anxiety, attention deficit hyperactivity disorder, hypertension and more. Poor breathing habits can even change the physical structure of our skeletons, depleting essential minerals and weakening our bones."

We lose about 12 percent of our lung capacity by the time we are 50 years old, and then the decline speeds up. Harvard Health Publishing, as of March 2016, makes the point, "All of us are born with the knowledge of how to fully engage the diaphragm to take deep, refreshing breaths. As we get older, however, we get out of the habit. Everything from the stresses of everyday life to the practice of 'sucking in' the stomach for a trimmer waistline encourages us to gradually shift to shallower, less satisfying chest breathing." But with proper breathing techniques we can reverse this trend.

The science behind these findings is not recent. Nestor discloses the following in his research article, "In the 1980s, researchers with the Framingham Study, a 70-year research program focused on heart disease, gathered two decades of data from 5,200 subjects, crunched the numbers and discovered that the greatest indicator of life span wasn't genetics, diet or the amount of daily exercise, as many had suspected. It was lung capacity.

Larger lungs equaled longer lives. Because big lungs allow us to get more air in with fewer breaths. They save the body from a lot of unnecessary wear and tear."

With information like this, it begins to make you wonder why this isn't discussed more openly in the news, at the doctor's office, in our schools, or in the case of those who study the martial arts. Breathing is, of course, brought up during martial arts training, but it tends to take a back seat to topics such as fighting, bag training, weapons training, and kata or forms. Quite frankly, the research noted previously should cause all martial artists to consider reversing the order of importance in their training curriculums.

We must be willing to let go of expectations, stay humble and open-minded, and accept there is still so much more to learn. Proper breathing comes with understanding of proper diaphragmatic breathing. According to the Cleveland Clinic website, diaphragmatic breathing is intended to help you use the diaphragm correctly while breathing in order to: strengthen the diaphragm, decrease the work of breathing by slowing your breathing rate, decrease oxygen demand, and use less effort and energy to breathe.

Utilizing breath, posture, and movement together in tandem helps to create a healthy body that is energetic and free from pain. Combining these three elements creates a dynamic effect of improved health, strength, and freedom of movement.

When you combine breath and movement, you should not focus on power but rather staying relaxed, so circulation of blood is improved. So, when karate systems apply dynamic muscle tension to the breathing that is forced and not relaxed, circulation of the blood is restricted. The focus should be on proper breathing coupled with controlled movement, which serves to train your connective tissue including the fascia, tendons, and ligaments of your body. When you look at the average age of lifelong Tai Chi practitioners, then you must figure they are doing something right.

———————◆———————

The most efficient and effective manner of movement ... is accomplished by the level of coordination between mind, body, and breath, as the movements are performed.

ALL ARTS ARE GOOD

"All bottles are good." That's what the founder of Isshinryu Karate, Tatsuo Shimabukuro, told his students one day after he posed a question to them. There were several bottles lined up and, pointing to them, he asked, "Which bottle is best?" After several guesses by selecting specific choices – the tallest one, the widest one, the one with the largest opening – Shimabukuro noted that they are all good in their own way. He alluded to the fact that all techniques serve a purpose; thus, the debate about which one is the best quickly becomes an exercise in futility. Similarly, the same could be said of the various martial arts styles and systems.

Taking up the martial arts is a very personal endeavor and the reasons behind such an undertaking – which is meant to be for life – are highly diversified. It is next to impossible to find a system of martial arts that has everything you need. The development of any system of martial arts stems from the collective experiences of the founder(s) and represent those techniques and concepts that they felt were important and effective. Furthermore, each style represents the curriculum of training that the founder(s) wished for their students to learn to pass along to future students to keep the legacy of that system alive and well. Because of the diverse nature and abilities of all those historical figures in martial arts, coupled with the array of potential reasons to study martial arts, it is useless to concern ourselves with the topic of which system or style is the best.

Essentially, you train in a particular system of martial arts depending on which one you enjoy practicing and the one in which you truly love to participate. And the choice becomes further dependent, over time, upon age and other considerations such as the number of martial arts available in any given area. At the core of anyone's interest or desire to train in the martial arts is the intent to improve oneself – physically, mentally, and spiritually. As such, it would be entirely inappropriate to judge anyone or ridicule them on the style in which they choose to train. All arts are good since the idea is to use them to better oneself and those around them.

It seems the need to be authoritative, even considering the personal reasons and good intentions of others to train in martial arts, remains for some. Social media such as Facebook is filled with posts where people continuously knock other styles and people. I see them constantly, and it even includes well-respected exponents of the arts and respected authors on the subject of martial arts. Everyone wants the last say or the ultimate word on what is correct or who has the true lineage of a particular system.

The world is too populated and diverse. There's room for everyone. Besides, taking the time to prepare an extended post on social media or discussing with others about how someone else is wrong or they are not the true martial art cannot possibly be a productive exercise for yourself.

I may be naïve, but for me one of the tenets of martial arts is to bring out the best in myself and others. The best way to accomplish that mindset is to keep my actions and words positive. This is not only something for martial artists to strive for – this is also something our world in general is badly lacking. For anyone considering taking up the martial arts, pay close attention to how the instructor and students discuss not only their art but other arts. If degrading other systems or constant complaining occurs, keep looking.

I, for one, respect anyone trying to improve themselves with whatever their chosen path may be. I see people in the gym who come from all walks of life and all shapes and sizes. Nobody has the right or the authority to question what they are doing. They are in there working on themselves and seeking something better in life.

Getting into the gym is ten times more than what the average person is willing to put forth anyway. God bless them. This is what we as martial artists need to strive for – acknowledging everyone for their commitment and effort to study the martial arts and strive to keep the legacy of their instructor and their respective system going for future generations.

We need to remove any sort of elitist mentality and exist in tandem with others. My first publication, *Sensei's Final Lessons*, was the story of my late Kendo sensei's final years and some of the lessons he imparted before his passing. He was a Korean who studied extensively in Japan during his lifetime. I asked a well-known author to review my draft and consider writing a Foreword or maybe a comment for the cover. His reaction was interesting.

He made it clear that he could not find in any Japanese records the name of my sensei or the Japanese master with whom he trained with while in Japan. He made it evidently clear that likely the Kendo that I was studying didn't have a validated lineage. This all-knowing reaction from this author, who I respect immensely based upon his array of publications, was disappointing. I can assure everyone the Kendo I trained in under Duk Yeong Kim was quite legitimate. So much so that a letter from Tokyo, Japan in 2012 provides a thank you from one of Kim Sensei's longtime friends thanking me for the publication in honoring him.

Within the Order of Isshin-Ryu Martial Arts, we have as one of our codes: *Things aren't always as they seem.* This highly respected author who reviewed my book did not know me, nor took the time to understand my position or the quality of my Kendo training. Yet he responded in a questioning tone to a fellow martial artist. It's easy to judge others and make assumptions, which often turn out false. Better to take the high road and realize all arts are good.

TRAINING: SOLO VS. GROUP

Depending on your sport or activity, the training and practice involved will likely be a mix of solo outings and group participation or at the very least with others around you doing the same. Team sports require the collective efforts and practice of others to make the sport function properly; but even then, there are times when solo practice is needed to improve your skills.

For example, in baseball not every player on the team is a pitcher. Therefore, practicing on your own the skills needed to improve your pitching performance has no bearing on the player who is the designated hitter. They need to work on their hitting skills apart from those who play a position on the infield or outfield, and so forth. Even in those situations, however, practice will likely include others present to help your efforts and ensure your practices are completed with everything you need.

In martial arts, the optimum scenario to improve your skills would be a group setting. This is especially true regarding ranks below black belt since martial arts not only involves learning and perfecting physical techniques, but there are also many standard rules of conduct within the dojo that adheres to historical aspects of the martial arts.

Without being in a group setting and following along with others more experienced, you would likely have trouble learning all those rules in the first place. The group environment in martial arts provides instant feedback and validation that what you are doing is either correct or not in line with what everyone else is doing. If the latter is the case, either the instructor or a higher ranked student can quickly notice and jump in to provide some adjustments, guidance, and explanation to get you on course.

The group setting is also beneficial in that you can gain inspiration from observing others more experienced than yourself. Martial arts are unique in that the group setting is a melting pot of various skill levels, whereas a team sport typically includes participants that are close in age, skill level, and experience.

Even in a martial arts school that offers classes for children, there are typically instructors and maybe several higher ranked student assistants that are much older that provide a good example of how an experienced martial artist should perform.

Regardless of whether it's an adult or children's class, there are varying degrees of skill levels included. Beginners quickly decipher who it is within class that they want to emulate with their movements and performance. Having that group atmosphere with highly skilled martial artists can create an energy that can keep you motivated and on track to ongoing improvement.

From time-to-time, reflect on your experiences within the group setting. Often, complacency can set in when you are around the same people over and over again. You say to yourself, "I'm doing well in class with the things we are training on, so I think I got it down." This type of thinking can lead to some problems.

For example, when sparring with the same people, you may get used to what others are doing and unconsciously fall into stagnation with your own skills. Or you work on specific drills from another system and think that you got it when you've only scratched the surface. It may be a good idea to visit other schools and train in a newer environment with others who you don't know so well.

There could also be a tendency to rely on the group environment too much. In other words, it becomes a habit that the only time some people train is when there is an actual class held. These people can't seem to train by themselves, or they don't try new things like visiting other schools, or attend seminars, or try another system to complement their main style unless someone they know goes with them.

As for solo training, martial arts literally demands it. But for many, this presents a problem. The group or class environment is comfortable so how do you adapt and train on your own? For many, the concept of setting aside time outside of regular classes is too much of a strain on daily agendas. Work, hobbies, and life in general tends to get in the way. Families can understand that twice a week from 6:00 – 8:00 pm is martial arts time. But any other time you wish to work on your martial arts is simply out of the question to them. For some, there are just so many problems to deal with to train solo on your martial arts skills.

Problems however, present an opportunity to grow. Motivational speaker Tony Robbins once said, "Problems make us better." And pastor Joel Osteen makes the point, "Our difficulties improve us more than our successes."

The bottom line is, if you value your martial arts, you will find a way to train by yourself. Excuses are the lazy man's way to normalcy. You may have valid reasons for being unable to train at certain times; however, valid reasons and excuses are two different things.

My father was a bodybuilder during the very early years of the sport. He competed at the 1963 AAU Mr. America contest. He once commented, "I never skipped a training day. Even if I'd hang out with my friends, I'd go home late at night and sneak into the basement while my family was asleep. I'd load the bar very slowly so I wouldn't make any noise and wake them up. I'd get my work in that way."

No excuses. Time of day or the fact you're on your own has no bearing. If you love it enough, you'll figure it out and find a way to get it done.

Frankly, training solo in martial arts is mandatory if you'll ever learn the lesson of perseverance. There's a reason why professional golfers go to the driving range, even after they have a spectacular round of golf. They love the process of working on their craft, and they want to lock in their muscle memory whatever worked on that day.

Martial arts are no different. What is working in the group setting must be worked by yourself, on your own, to lock in the proper sensation of what a good technique is supposed to feel like. You must simply enjoy the repetition of the strikes, blocks, kata, or forms, stretching — all of it. You must work on the problems you're facing in the dojo at home; otherwise, progression will suffer. You'll never understand how to figure things out and overcome difficulties both in your martial arts, and in life.

STAY UNCOMFORTABLE

Comfort has the power to weaken and destroy our motivations. It forces us to forget what it took – mentally and physically – to get to where we are today. Comfort gives us an excuse, and easy 'out' to staying right we are whether that's metaphorical or actual. If there is anything in life that leads us to improve or to reach our stated goals, it's staying uncomfortable. There is no way around it.

If everything in life were easy and comfortable, we'd all be successful as this is what we tend to gravitate towards as human beings – the easy road. But as the elite bodybuilder, eight-time Mr. Olympia Ronnie Coleman once said, "Ain't nobody gonna give you nothin."

The only thing proven in this life is hard work. So, gauge yourself now and then. If you're becoming comfortable, your progression and improvement is likely falling off.

Whenever we see a highly skilled athlete, or martial artist, or even those successful in business or the arts, we comment how talented they are or how effortless they appear in their performances. Everyone appreciates the result. The process is what is unseen yet is far more important.

Watching an interview of golfer Tiger Woods from years ago, he was commenting on his day-to-day training program. He rattled off a bunch of activities for a given day. From running to weightlifting to playing tennis – as well as a round of golf – his day seemed non-stop from sunup to sundown. He noted how arduous and painful it was at times. However, he realized that without sticking to a plan and dealing with various degrees of discomfort in his training, that progress would surely stall in his professional game.

Those who understand what it takes to improve know that accepting discomfort is part of the deal. It becomes a part of life. This doesn't apply strictly to athletics. Think of your education. To improve you will face discomfort.

In writing this book it took a disciplined approach. Writing whenever I felt like it simply would not get the job done. A plan needed to be crafted and adhered to for any level of progression to occur. Was it uncomfortable? Absolutely. In order to stick to the plan and the goal to complete the book, other things needed to be put on hold.

For a specific timeframe every day, the only thing that mattered was working on this book. It's uncomfortable knowing that many other things need my attention. There are many other things I'd rather be doing; however, those other things would stand in the way of my goal. To achieve my stated goal, I knew that I had to stay uncomfortable and work until the goal was met.

Thinking about being uncomfortable means you are thinking big and are not putting limits on yourself. Why would you want to think small? We were all made to do big things if we set our minds to it. Of course, the 'big' we all strive for is relative; however, if we keep our goals small, we won't really need to deal with much difficulty and discomfort.

What if someone told you that you were only capable of small things? That your limit or potential was very low. Would life be exciting and worth looking forward to?

But we never know or are told what the ceiling is for each of us. That's what makes life worth living – knowing that we can set a very high mark for ourselves and, if we're willing to work hard and deal with the discomfort, that we can reach those limits and beyond. As author Gary Keller points out in his book *The One Thing*, "Big is a placeholder for what you might call a leap of possibility. It's the office intern visualizing the boardroom or a penniless immigrant imagining a business revolution. It's about bold ideas that might threaten your comfort zones but simultaneously reflect your greatest opportunities. Believing in big frees you to ask different questions, follow different paths, and try new things."

For most of us, asking different questions, following different paths, and trying new things can make us extremely uncomfortable. But that is precisely the areas that provide true growth and progression in our lives.

In the martial arts arena, it's a matter of telling yourself that you never really 'got it'. There's always something more to learn and experience. You may learn a new series of techniques or a new form; however, there is so much more to explore than merely memorizing those movements.

Sometimes students in martial arts fall into the trap of saying, "Yeah okay, I got those moves. What's next?" They want to stay comfortable. Rather, the approach should be to drill those movements over and over and realize there's more layers to explore than what meets the eye.

Stay uncomfortable by continuing to work the moves and researching them from all angles. Furthermore, how you make specific movements and techniques work now will likely not apply 10-15 years in the future. Your mind and body will change; therefore, your execution and understanding of the same movements will change. If you become comfortable, you will likely forget about working those movements and your skill and knowledge will be lost.

Stay uncomfortable – progression and improvement with anything in life depends on it.

REFLECT

Life is a continual, ever-changing process of collective experiences, ideas, hard work, and relationships that [hopefully] enriches both sides. A key ingredient to this ongoing process is reflecting upon events that unfold in your life – whether they were recent or in the distant past. Yet, how often is this a concerted effort? What importance is placed on time for reflection when life is constantly speeding at you coupled with the electronic diversions of today such as smartphones, Instagram, Netflix, and video games? Our society is losing this critical assessment tool, and the impact is not only on the younger generations but everyone, it's becoming more apparent every day.

It is said that history should be taught in school, so we don't repeat the mistakes of our ancestors. Should this not apply to our own lives as well? My older daughter struggled with an elective astronomy course in college, and she ultimately needed to drop the class. A few semesters later, it turned out she needed this same course to fulfill her credits for transfer into Penn State. And to make it more challenging, she needed to take the class over a six-week summer session. I encouraged her to reflect on the prior experience for this class. Review what was challenging and what didn't quite work out. Reflect on the teaching style of the professor and what could be some of the pitfalls to look out for. In doing so, she was able to adjust her approach to the class and passed the summer offering with flying colors.

Reflection provides the opportunity to enlighten yourself as to what works, what doesn't work, and what could be adjusted to improve something you are currently doing. In Ben Hogan's book *Five Lessons: The Modern Fundamentals of Golf* he documents when he realized that he didn't need to over-obsess about every little part of his golf swing. He noted, "I had stopped trying to do a great many difficult things perfectly because it had become clear in my mind that this ambitious over-thoroughness was neither possible nor advisable, or even necessary. All you needed to groove [the swing] were the fundamental movements – and there weren't so many of them."

This realization came to Hogan after many years of competitive golf and continual reflection upon his craft. This enlightened frame of mind from his process of reflection led to a long string of successes, including his iconic 1950 victory at the U.S. Open at Merion, Pennsylvania while coming back from serious injury after a major car accident.

Whether you're a martial artist, an athlete, or someone who wants to improve some aspect of their lives, you need to continually study and reflect to learn about yourself. This process never ends. Walther von Krenner makes this point in his book *Following the Martial Path* by stating, "Have you ever noticed how much of our practice focuses on studying? We are not members, adherents, patients, or clients. We are students. The emphasis is on learning, and to learn we must be open and ready to learn ourselves. Zen master Dogen reminds us that study is self-empowerment. No one can study for you, and you cannot bypass it and buy the result. You have to do it for yourself. This requires discipline. It requires constant reflection, because without reflection, there can be no growth."

Carve out time in your busy schedule to reflect. The process has proven time and again to be one of the best sources to learn about yourself. Don't just engage in a particular martial art, sport, or activity of interest. Study it. Read books on the subject. Consider reading topics of similar interest. All the sources used for this book are not martial arts specific, yet they all contributed to my personal growth in a profound manner.

Stop comparing yourself to others, or especially to your former self. Comparison will only steal your joy and take away any chance of noticing areas of self-improvement. Reflecting on what you're doing can uncover this self-destructive behavior, among others. Figure out what works best for you to formally reflect upon your training or actions.

It's no different than finding time for prayer, finding time to reach out to a friend or someone in need, or working into your schedule time for relaxation. You need to consciously put into your schedule the activity and pursue it without fail. Disciplined actions tend to lead towards results – and reflection is a tool that you cannot afford to leave in the toolbox.

PHOTO CREDITS

Location	Subject	Credit
Chapter 1	Author	Britteni Popp
Chapter 3	Kayla Popp	Sheryl Z Photography
Chapter 4	books	Author
Chapter 11	Author	Britteni Popp
Chapter 14	Shodo by Author	Author
Chapter 20	medal / Keystone State Games	Author
Chapter 22	Author	John Costanzo
Chapter 25	Author	Britteni Popp
Chapter 28	Britteni Popp	Author

SOURCES

Book Sources

An Old Man's Way, by Jason S.D. Perry - ©2018 by Jason Perry. Published by Apsos Publishing.

Double Blessing, by Mark Batterson - ©2019 by Mark Batterson. Published by Multnomah, a division of Penguin Random House LLC.

Following the Martial Path: Lessons and Stories from a Lifetime of Training in Budo and Zen, by Walther G. von Krenner with Ken Jeremiah - ©2016 Walther G. von Krenner, published by Tambuli Media

He Chose the Nails, by Max Lucado - ©2000 by Max Lucado. Published by Thomas Nelson, Inc.

In a Pit With a Lion on a Snowy Day, by Mark Batterson - ©2006 by Mark Batterson. Published by Multnomah.

It's How You Play the Game – The 12 Leadership Principles of Dean Smith, by David Chadwick - ©2015 David Chadwick, published by Harvest House Publishers.

Jesus – The God Who Knows Your Name, by Max Lucado - ©2020 by Max Lucado. Published by Thomas Nelson, Inc.

Kendo: The Definitive Guide, by Hiroshi Ozawa - ©1997 by Hiroshi Ozawa. English translation ©1997 by Kodansha International Ltd. Published by Kodansha International Ltd.

More to Your Story, by Max Lucado - ©2011, 2016 by Max Lucado. Published by Thomas Nelson.

Moving Toward Stillness, by Dave Lowry - ©2000 by Dave Lowry. Published by Tuttle Publishing.

Old School, Essays on Japanese Martial Traditions, by Ellis Amdur - ©2002 Ellis Amdur, published by Edgework

Order of Isshin-Ryu: One Family, One Dojo, by Dan Popp - ©2018 by Dan Popp. Published by Kamel Press, LLC.

Order of Isshin-Ryu Student Handbook, ©1971-2019 by Order of Isshin-Ryu.

Shorin-Ryu Karatedo – Temple of the Young Trees, by Steven Ballenger - ©2018 by Steven Ballenger.

Suffering: Gospel Hope When Life Doesn't Make Sense, by Paul David Tripp - ©2018 by Paul David Tripp. Published by Crossway.

The Book of Five Rings, by Miyamoto Musashi, Translated by Thomas Cleary - ©1993, 1994 by Thomas Cleary. Published by Shambhala Publications, Inc.

The Modern Fundamentals of Golf, by Ben Hogan and Herbert Warren Wind - ©1957 by Ben Hogan. Published by Simon & Schuster, Inc.

The One Thing: The Surprisingly Simple Truth Behind Extraordinary Results, by Gary Keller and Jay Papasan - ©2012 Rellek Publishing Partners, Ltd. Published by Bard Press.

The Power of Positive Thinking, by Norman Vincent Peale - ©1952, 1956 by Prentice-Hall, Inc. Copyright renewed ©1980 by Norman Vincent Peale. Published by Touchstone, A Division of Simon & Schuster, Inc.

The Spark and the Grind, by Erik Wahl - ©2017 by Art is Freedom, LLC. Portfolio / Penguin.

The Writing Warrior, by Laraine Herring - ©2010 Laraine Herring, published by Shambhala Publications, Inc.

Zen in the Martial Arts, by Joe Hyams - ©1979 by Joe Hyams. Published by Bantam Books.

Zen Word, Zen Calligraphy, by Eido Tai Shimano and Kogetsu Tani - ©1990, 1995 by Theseus Verlag, Zurich, Munich. Published by Shambhala Publications, Inc.

Internet Sources

Google searches and internet sources provided historical photographs, articles and maps presented in this text.

Chi-Ryu Jiujitsu

www.wakinghands.com

Cleveland Clinic

www.musclememory.com/show.php?c=Mr+America+-+AAU&y=1963

Wikipedia - https://en.wikipedia.org/wiki/Kata

Wikipedia - https://en.wikipedia.org/wiki/Tatsuo_Shimabuku

YouTube
3 Kata Secrets. By Iain Abernethy and Jesse Enkamp.

ABOUT THE AUTHOR

Dan began the study of Isshin Ryu Karate in 1982. Currently holding the rank of Nana-dan (7th degree black belt), Dan was named the 2008 Male Instructor of the Year by the International Isshinryu Hall of Fame and subsequently inducted into the Isshinryu Hall of Fame in July 2013. He currently serves on the Board of Directors for the Order of Isshin-Ryu, founded by Toby Cooling in 1971. Dan's training in martial arts is diverse, and he holds the following yudansha ranks: Order of Isshin-Ryu (7th degree), Manasyu Karate (5th degree), SMP Arnis (4th degree), Kendo (4th degree), and Chi-Ryu Jiujitsu (1st degree).

He studied the art of Shodo, or Japanese calligraphy, from his Kendo sensei Duk Yeong Kim. Although his Kendo/ Shodo sensei passed away in 2007, Dan continues to practice Shodo to honor his teacher. His Shodo works have been exhibited at Mulberry Art Studios in Lancaster, PA and at Gallery at Second in Harrisburg, PA. Nationally, his commissioned works can be found in Arizona, California, Delaware, Florida, Georgia, Kentucky, Maryland, Nevada, Oregon, Puerto Rico, Texas, and Virginia. His international commissions include Australia and Canada.

Dan has also promoted two tournaments for the World Kumdo Association (Korean Kendo) in Harrisburg, Pennsylvania. The 1st World Kumdo Association tournament held in 1998 and the 2nd U.S. Open Kumdo Championships held in 2001 where he received the Kumdo Ambassador Award.

He is the author of three books which can be ordered through Amazon or the publisher in both print and Kindle:

Sensei's Final Lessons – A Memoir, published in 2012 by Outskirts Press.

The Floating Brush, Learning Japanese Calligraphy from a Kendo Master, published in 2014 by Kamel Press.

Order of Isshin Ryu – One Family, One Dojo, published in 2018 by Kamel Press.

Sensei Popp has a publication in process to present the martial art of Chi-Ryu Jiujitsu, founded by Masters Isham Latimer, John Costanzo, and John McDonald. Dan is also an editorial contributor for Bugeisha magazine, a quarterly publication focusing on the traditional aspects of the martial arts.

A 1994 graduate of The Pennsylvania State University with a B.S. in Professional Accountancy, Dan was employed in 1999 by the National Credit Union Administration where he still serves as a federal examiner specializing in IT audits. He holds several IT and information security audit certifications including CISA, CGEIT, and CRISC. He resides in Harrisburg, PA with his two daughters, Britteni and Kayla.

www.ingramcontent.com/pod-product-compliance
Lightning Source LLC
Chambersburg PA
CBHW031134090426
42738CB00008B/1080